THE BOOK OF
PIZZAS & PASTA

250 STEP-BY-STEP RECIPES

EASY AND DELICIOUS APPETIZERS, SOUPS, SNACKS AND MAIN DISHES

THE BOOK OF
PIZZAS & PASTA

250 STEP-BY-STEP RECIPES
EASY AND DELICIOUS APPETIZERS, SOUPS, SNACKS AND MAIN DISHES

CRESCENT BOOKS
New York

Published by Salamander Books Ltd
129-137 York Way, London N7 9LG, United Kingdom

© Salamander Books 1991

Recipes and photographs on the following pages
are the copyright of Merehurst Press,
and credited as follows:
3 (bottom picture), 49, 50, 51, 52, 53, 54, 55, 56, 57, 58, 59, 60,
61, 62, 63, 64, 65, 66, 67, 68, 69, 70, 71, 72, 73, 74, 75, 76, 77,
78, 79, 80, 81, 82, 83, 84, 85, 86, 87, 88, 89, 90, 91, 92, 93, 94, 95

All correspondence concerning the content of this volume
should be addressed to Salamander Books Ltd.

This 1991 edition published by Crescent Books, distributed
by Outlet Book Company, Inc., a Random House Company,
225 Park Avenue South, New York, New York 10003.

Printed and bound in Italy

ISBN 0 517 06148 1

87654321

─────────────── CREDITS ───────────────

Designer: Sara Cooper

Contributing authors: Sarah Bush and Lesley Mackley

Typeset by: Maron Graphics Ltd., Wembley

Colour separation by: J. Film Process Ltd., Bangkok, Thailand and
Kentscan Ltd.

Photographer: Jon Stewart, assisted by Kay Small
and Alister Thorpe

CONTENTS

PIZZAS

THE HISTORY OF PIZZAS

In Naples one summer, around the late 1800s, Queen Margherita of Savoy was residing with her family in Capodimonte Park. She had heard a lot about pizza and decided to try it for herself. The local pizza maker was summoned and he served her a pizza with a newly invented topping. From then on, the tomato, mozzarella cheese and fresh basil pizza has been known as Pizza Margherita.

Until this time, pizza had been sold in the streets to people at breakfast, lunch and dinner. It was cut from a large tray that had been cooked in the baker's oven and had a simple topping of mushrooms and anchovies.

As pizza became more popular, stalls were set up where the dough was shaped as customers ordered. Various toppings were invented. The tomato, which had arrived from the New World, was one of the most popular. The stalls soon developed into the pizzeria, an open air place for people to congregate, eat, drink and talk. This has gradually become the pizza parlors we have today, although the flavor of a pizza made, baked and cooked in the open air is unbeatable.

The dough for the pizza has been baked in other countries of the Mediterranean for just as long. The French have their own pissaladière recipe; for the Middle Eastern countries it's pita bread and Spain uses the dough as a pastry for spicy savory fillings. Even as far as China the same dough is steamed and served as individual stuffed snacks.

Although enjoying steady and constant popularity, it seems the pizza is now becoming a sophisticated, fashionable food with exotic toppings and unusual shapes. Who knows what will happen to the pizza in years to come!

INGREDIENTS

The traditional pizzas of Italy rely on the wonderful Mediterranean ingredients that are so plentiful—sun-ripened tomatoes, golden olive oil, fresh herbs and cheeses are the most well-known, but all sorts of other ingredients can be used as well.

Olive oil is indispensable for making genuine Italian flavored pizza.

Olives that are both green and ripe are used. Olive pulp is made from crushed ripe olives and is available in jars from gourmet shops and delicatessens.

Capers are buds from a flowering plant. They have a delicious, though distinct flavor, so use with care.

Oregano (wild marjoram) is used on many pizzas. Use fresh whenever possible.

Thyme, highly aromatic, can be used fresh or dried.

Parsley, both flat and curly, is used. Use only fresh parsley.

Basil is the most aromatic of all the Italian herbs. Use fresh whenever possible.

Sweet marjoram is added to pizzas after cooking.

Sage has a strong pronounced flavor. Use with care.

Mint should only be used fresh.

Black peppercorns should be freshly ground as the aroma disappears very quickly from the ready-ground type.

Nutmeg should be used freshly ground for the best flavor.

Chiles may be used fresh or dried.

Dried tomatoes in oil have an unusual, distinct flavor and are available from gourmet shops and delicatessens.

Cheeses. Mozzarella, Parmesan, Pecorino, Gorgonzola and Ricotta cheese are all used in pizzas. (Parmesan and Pecorino are at their best when freshly grated.)

EQUIPMENT

Flat pizza pan: Metal is essential to conduct the heat and ensure that the bottom of the pizza is crisp.

Baking sheet: This can be used as an alternative to the flat pizza pan, however, a rim should be formed at the edge of the dough to keep the filling in place.

Rectangular pan or jellyroll pan: Use this for making the traditional Roman pizza or any pizza that you wish to serve cut in squares.

Deep pizza pan: Use for the thick crust pizza. A cake pan or pie pan may be used instead.

Pizza cutter: This makes the job of cutting a pizza far easier than using a knife.

TRADITIONAL PIZZA DOUGH — — VARIATIONS —

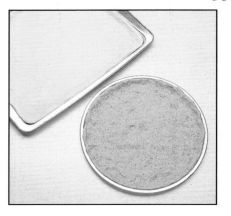

If preferred, bake in a 14" x 10" jellyroll pan, or as 4 individual pizzas.

2-3/4 cups bread flour
1 teaspoon salt
1 teaspoon active dried yeast
1 teaspoon sugar
About 3/4 cup warm water (110F, 45C)
1 tablespoon olive oil

Sift flour and salt into a medium bowl.

Herb or Nut Pizza Dough: Knead 2 tablespoons chopped fresh herbs (or 1 tablespoon dried herbs) into the dough. If preferred, knead 1 ounce chopped walnuts into the dough.

In a small bowl, combine yeast, sugar and 1/4 cup water; leave until frothy. Add yeast liquid to flour with remaining water and oil. Mix to a soft dough; knead on a floured surface 10 minutes until smooth. Place in a greased bowl; cover with plastic wrap. Let rise in a warm place 45 minutes or until doubled in size.

Whole-Wheat Pizza Dough: Use 2-1/4 cups whole-wheat flour and 1/4 cup wheat germ. Add extra water as required to form a soft dough.

Punch down dough and knead briefly. Oil a 12-inch pizza pan. Place dough in center of pan; press out to edges with your knuckles. Pinch up edges to make a rim. Use as directed in recipe.

Cornmeal Pizza Dough: Use 2-1/4 cups bread flour and 1/3 cup cornmeal.

— POTATO PIZZA DOUGH —

Press potato through a sieve into flour; stir in yeast and remaining water.

1 (5-oz.) potato
2-3/4 cups bread flour
1 teaspoon salt
1 teaspoon active dried yeast
1 teaspoon sugar
3/4 cup warm water (110F, 45C)

Scrub the unpeeled potato.

Mix to a soft dough; and knead on a lightly floured surface 10 minutes until smooth. Place in a greased bowl; cover with plastic wrap. Let rise in a warm place about 45 minutes until doubled in size.

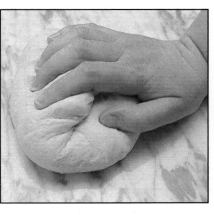

Boil in the skin 30 to 40 minutes or until tender when pierced with a fork. Drain and cool enough to remove the skin.

Punch down dough and knead briefly. Oil a 12-inch pizza pan. Place dough in the center of pan and press out to edges with your knuckles. Pinch up edges to make a rim. Use as directed in recipe.

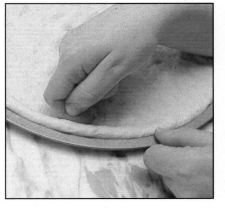

Sift flour and salt into a medium bowl. In a small bowl, cream fresh yeast with a little of the water and put in a warm place until frothy. If using dried active yeast, whisk together with the sugar and little water and set aside. If using easy blend yeast, mix into flour and salt at this stage (do not add any liquid).

Variations: Knead 2 tablespoons chopped fresh herbs or 2 tablespoons freshly grated Parmesan cheese into the dough.

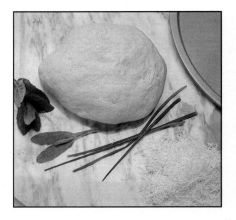

PAN PIZZA DOUGH

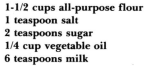

1-1/4 cups bread flour
1-1/4 cups all-purpose flour
1 teaspoon salt
1 teaspoon active dried yeast
1 teaspoon sugar
3/4 cup warm water (110F, 45C)

Make dough as for Traditional Pizza Dough, page 10. When dough has doubled in size, punch down and knead briefly.

Thoroughly oil a deep 10-inch pizza pan or cake pan. Place dough in the center of pan and press out to edges with your knuckles.

Cover with plastic wrap; let rise in a warm place about 1-1/2 hours or until almost to the top of pan. Use as directed in recipe.

CRUMBLE PIZZA DOUGH

1-1/2 cups all-purpose flour
1 teaspoon salt
2 teaspoons sugar
1/4 cup vegetable oil
6 teaspoons milk

Sift flour, salt and sugar into a medium bowl. Whisk oil and milk together in a measuring cup; pour onto flour mixture.

Stir with a fork until mixture is crumbly but still moist. It will not form a dough.

Press mixture onto bottom and up side of a deep 10-inch pizza pan or cake pan. Use as directed in recipe.

QUICK PIZZA DOUGH

1 cup whole-wheat flour
1 cup all purpose flour
2 teaspoons baking powder
Salt and pepper
1/4 cup butter or margarine
About 2/3 cup milk

Put flours and baking powder into a large bowl. Season to taste with salt and pepper. Add butter or margarine and rub in with fingertips until mixture resembles bread crumbs.

Stir in enough milk to form a dough. Turn onto a lightly floured surface; knead briefly.

Roll out dough to a 10-inch circle. Transfer to a greased baking sheet. Use as directed in recipe.

Variation: Stir 2 tablespoons chopped fresh parsley into crumb mixture before adding milk.

Pizza Carcoifi

1 recipe Traditional Pizza Dough, shaped and ready for topping, page 8

Topping:
2 tablespoons Tomato Topping, page 12
1/2 cup (2 oz.) shredded Fontina cheese
1 (6 oz.) jar marinated artichoke hearts
8 sun-dried tomatoes in oil
Salt and pepper
Parsley leaves, to garnish

Preheat oven to 425F (220C). Spread the dough with Tomato Topping. Sprinkle with cheese.

Drain artichokes, reserving oil. Drain tomatoes. Slice artichokes and arrange over the cheese. Chop tomatoes roughly and sprinkle over the artichokes. Season to taste with salt and pepper. Sprinkle with 1 to 2 tablespoons of the reserved oil.

Bake 20 minutes until dough is golden. Garnish with parsley. Makes 4 servings.

Pizza Napolitana

1 recipe Traditional Pizza Dough, shaped and ready for topping, page 8

Topping:
3 tablespoons olive oil
1 pound tomatoes
1 garlic clove, crushed
Salt and pepper
8 ounces mozzarella cheese
1 (2-oz.) can anchovy fillets, drained
1 tablespoon chopped fresh oregano
Oregano leaves, to ganish

Preheat oven to 425F (220C). Brush dough with 1 tablespoon oil. Place tomatoes in a bowl. Pour enough boiling water over tomatoes to cover. Let stand 1 minute. Drain, peel and coarsely chop. Spread over dough. Sprinkle with garlic; season to taste with salt and pepper.

Slice cheese thinly. Arrange over tomatoes. Chop anchovies and sprinkle over cheese. Sprinkle with oregano and remaining oil. Bake 20 minutes until cheese has melted and dough is crisp and golden. Garnish with oregano leaves. Serve at once. Makes 4 servings.

Pizza Margherita

1 recipe Traditional Pizza Dough, page 8

Tomato Topping:
1 pound tomatoes, peeled, see left or 1 (16-oz.) can tomatoes
2 tablespoons olive oil
1 onion, finely chopped
1 garlic clove, crushed
1 tablespoon tomato paste
1/2 teaspoon sugar
1 tablespoon chopped fresh basil
Salt and pepper

To Finish:
1 to 2 tablespoons olive oil
4 ounces mozzarella cheese
6 to 8 fresh basil leaves
Basil sprig, to garnish

Make Tomato Topping. Chop tomatoes, if using fresh. Heat oil in a medium saucepan. Add onion and garlic; cook until soft. Stir in tomatoes, tomato paste, sugar and basil. Season to taste with salt and pepper. Cover pan and simmer 30 minutes until thick.

Preheat oven to 425F (220C). Lightly grease a 12-inch pizza pan. Punch down dough and knead briefly. Place in prepared pan and press out to edges with your knuckles. Brush dough with 1 tablespoon oil. Spoon Tomato Topping over dough. Slice cheese thinly. Arrange over sauce. Sprinkle with salt and pepper to taste, 2 or 3 basil leaves and remaining oil. Bake 20 minutes until cheese has melted and dough is crisp and golden. Sprinkle with remaining basil leaves. Garnish with basil sprig. Serve at once. Makes 4 servings.

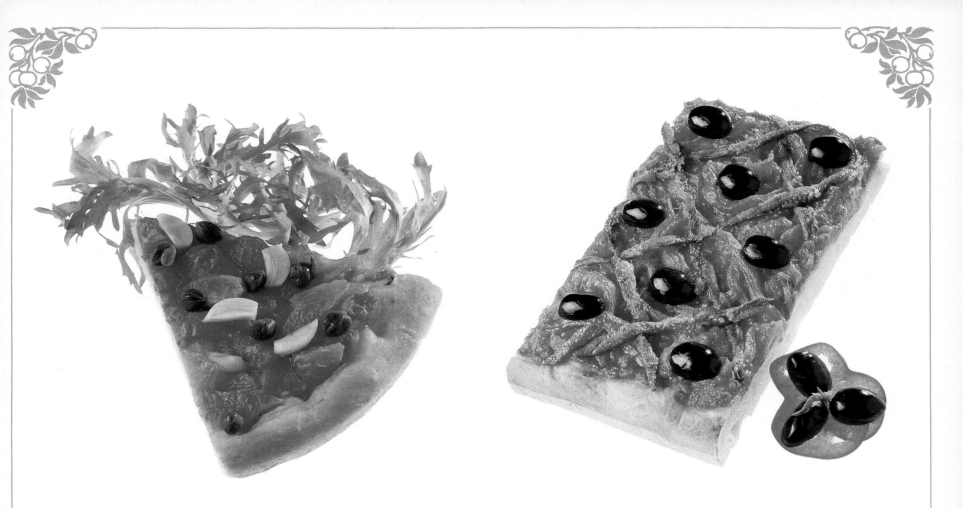

Pizza Marinara

1 recipe Traditional Pizza Dough, shaped
  and ready for topping, page 8

Topping:
3 tablespoons olive oil
8 ounces tomatoes, peeled, page 12
3 large garlic cloves
Salt and pepper
few capers, if desired

Preheat oven to 425F (220C). Brush
dough with 1 tablespoon oil.

Quarter tomatoes and discard seeds.
Chop coarsely and drain in a sieve.
Spread over dough. Cut garlic into
thick slices and sprinkle over tomatoes.

Season with salt and pepper. Sprinkle
with remaining oil. Bake 20 minutes
until dough is crisp and golden. Sprinkle with capers. Makes 4 servings.

Roman Pizza

1 recipe Traditional Pizza Dough, made up
  to end of step 2, page 8

Topping:
3 tablespoons olive oil
2 large onions, chopped
1 pound tomatoes, peeled, page 12, or 1
  (16-oz.) can tomatoes, drained, chopped
1 (6-oz.) can pimentos, drained
1 (2-oz.) can anchovy fillets
12 pitted ripe olives
Pimentos and olives, to garnish

Preheat oven to 425F (220C). Lightly
grease a 14" x 10" jellyroll pan. Punch
down dough and knead briefly. Place in
prepared pan; press out to edges with
your knuckles. Pinch up edges to make
a rim.

In a saucepan, heat 2 tablespoons oil.
Add onions; cook until soft. Chop
tomatoes, if fresh, add to pan and cook
2 minutes. Spoon over dough. Slice
pimentos in strips and arrange over
tomatoes. Drain anchovies, cut in half
lengthwise and arrange in a lattice pattern on top. Halve olives and place in
gaps. Sprinkle with remaining oil.

Bake 20 minutes until dough is crisp
and golden. Garnish with pimento and
olives. Makes 4 servings.

Four Seasons Pizza

1 recipe Traditional Pizza Dough, made up
  to end of step 2, page 8

Topping:
3 tablespoons olive oil
2 ounces button mushrooms
2 ounces prosciutto (Parma ham)
6 pitted ripe olives
4 canned artichoke hearts, drained
2 ounces mozzarella cheese
1 tomato, peeled, page 12
Salt and pepper

Preheat oven to 425F (220C). Lightly
grease a baking sheet. Punch down
dough and knead briefly. Place dough
on baking sheet. Press out with your
knuckles to a 10-inch circle. Brush
dough with a little oil.

Heat 2 tablespoons oil in a medium
saucepan. Add mushrooms; cook 5
minutes. Mark dough into 4 equal sections with a knife. Arrange mushrooms
over one section. Cut ham in strips and
chop olives; sprinkle over second section. Slice artichokes thinly. Arrange
over third section. Slice cheese and
tomato and arrange over fourth section. Season to taste with salt and pepper. Drizzle with remaining oil. Bake 20
minutes until dough is crisp and golden. Serve at once. Makes 4 servings.

Variation: Make this recipe as 4 individual pizzas, if preferred.

Spicy Pork & Pepper Pizza

1 recipe Traditional Pizza Dough, shaped
  and ready for topping, page 8

Topping:
2 tablespoons olive oil
1 recipe Tomato Topping, see page 12
1 cup (4 oz.) mozzarella cheese
3 to 4 Italian pork sausages
Salt and pepper
1 yellow bell pepper, chopped
2 tablespoons freshly grated Parmesan
  cheese
Chopped fresh parsley, to garnish

Preheat oven to 425F (220C). Brush
dough with 1 tablespoon oil. Spread
Tomato Topping over dough. Sprinkle
cheese on top. With a sharp knife, cut
skins from sausages and discard. Cut
meat into pieces; scatter over cheese.
Season to taste with salt and pepper.

Sprinkle with chopped bell pepper,
Parmesan cheese and remaining oil.
Bake 20 minutes until dough is crisp.
Garnish with parsley. Makes 4 servings.

Prosciutto & Olive Pizza

1 recipe Traditional Pizza Dough, shaped
   and ready for topping, page 8

Topping:
6 ounces mozzarella cheese
4 slices prosciutto
2 tablespoons olive pulp, see note
2 tablespoons olive oil
Salt and pepper

To Garnish:
Prosciutto
Few olives
Basil sprigs

Preheat oven to 425F (220C). Make the
topping. Cut cheese and prosciutto into
cubes. Place in bowl with olive pulp.
Mix together and moisten with a little
oil if dry. Spread over dough. Season to
taste with salt and pepper and sprinkle
with remaining oil. Bake 20 minutes
until dough is crisp and golden. Garnish with curls of prosciutto, olives and
basil sprigs. Makes 4 servings.

Note: Olive pulp may be bought in jars
from gourmet shops.

Italian Sausage Pizza

1 recipe Traditional Pizza Dough, shaped
   and ready for topping, page 8

Topping:
2 tablespoons olive oil
1 recipe Tomato Topping, page 12
2 ounces mushrooms, finely sliced
3 spicy Italian sausages
2 tablespoons freshly grated Pecorino
   cheese
Salt and pepper
Grated Pecorino cheese and flat-leaf
   parsley, to garnish

Preheat oven to 425F (220C). Brush
dough with 1 tablespoon oil. Spread
Tomato Topping over dough and
sprinkle with mushrooms. With a sharp
knife, cut skins from the sausages and
discard. Cut meat into pieces and arrange over mushrooms. Sprinkle with 2
tablespoons grated cheese. Season to
taste with salt and pepper.

Sprinkle remaining oil over top. Bake
20 minutes until dough is crisp and
golden. Serve garnished with additional grated Pecorino cheese and flat-leaf
parsley. Makes 4 servings.

Three Pepper Pizza

1 recipe Traditional Pizza Dough, shaped
   and ready for topping, page 8

Topping:
1 red pepper
1 yellow pepper
1 green pepper
2 tomatoes, peeled, page 12
3 tablespoons olive oil
1 onion, finely chopped
1 garlic clove, crushed
Salt and pepper
Pinch of dried leaf oregano
Oregano sprigs and olives, to garnish

Make the topping. Peel peppers: spear one at a time with a fork and hold over a gas flame for 5 to 10 minutes until black and blistered. Or, halve and seed peppers. Place under preheated grill until black. Peel skin off with a knife.

Chop red pepper; quarter, seed and chop tomatoes. Put in a saucepan with 2 tablespoons oil, onion and garlic. Cook until soft. Preheat oven to 425F (220C). Brush dough with a little oil.

Spread red pepper mixture over dough. Season to taste with salt and pepper. Sprinkle with oregano. Cut remaining peppers in strips. Arrange over pizza. Season to taste with salt and pepper. Drizzle with remaining oil. Bake 20 minutes until dough is crisp and golden. Garnish with oregano sprigs and olives. Makes 4 servings.

Four Cheese Pizza

1 recipe Traditional Pizza Dough, shaped
   and ready for topping, page 8

Topping:
2 tablespoons olive oil
2 ounces mozzarella cheese
2 ounces Gorgonzola cheese
2 ounces Fontina or Gruyère cheese
1/2 cup freshly grated Parmesan cheese
Salt and pepper
Chopped green onion and grated
   Parmesan cheese, to garnish

Preheat oven to 425F (220C). Brush dough with 1 tablespoon oil. Cut the first 3 cheeses into small cubes. Scatter over the dough. Sprinkle with Parmesan cheese; season to taste with salt and pepper. Drizzle with remaining oil.

Bake 20 minutes until cheese is melted and dough is crisp and golden. Garnish with green onion and additional Parmesan cheese. Makes 4 servings.

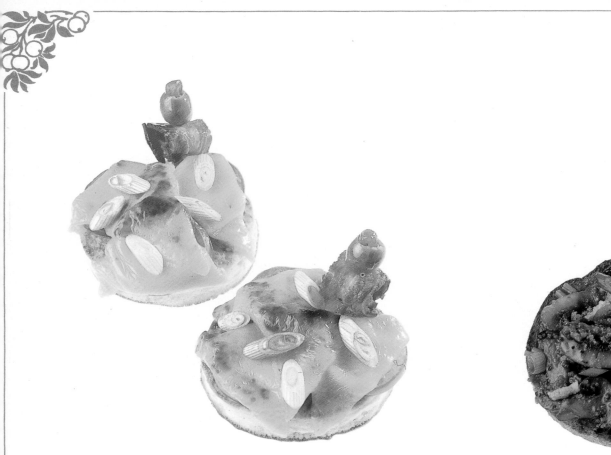

English Muffin Pizzas

4 English muffins, halved
1/4 cup butter
2 tablespoons anchovy paste
4 tomatoes, sliced
8 slices processed Cheddar cheese
4 green onions
Stuffed olives
8 slices bacon, cooked until almost crisp

Preheat broiler. Toast muffins.

In a bowl, beat butter and anchovy paste together. Spread a little on each muffin half. Arrange tomato slices on halves.

Cut cheese slices diagonally into 4 triangular shapes. Arrange on top of muffin halves. Broil until cheese melts. Slice green onions and sprinkle on top. Spear olives with wooden picks. Roll up bacon; secure each roll with a pick with an olive. Use to garnish pizzas. Makes 4 servings.

Spicy Mushroom Muffins

4 whole-wheat English muffins

Topping:
2 tablespoons vegetable oil
1 tablespoon grated gingerroot, if desired
12 ounces mushrooms, sliced
1 bunch green onions, sliced
2 teaspoons Worcestershire sauce
1/2 teaspoon Dijon-style mustard
Salt and pepper
Butter for spreading, if desired
Green onion brushes, to garnish

Preheat oven to 425F (220C). Split muffins. Toast on both sides.

Meanwhile make topping. Heat oil in a large saucepan. Add gingerroot, if desired and cook for 10 to 15 seconds, stirring.

Add mushrooms; cook, stirring, for 1 minute. Add green onions and continue to cook 10 seconds. Add Worcestershire sauce and mustard. Season to taste with salt and pepper. Butter muffins, if desired. Spoon mushroom mixture on top of muffins. Bake 2 to 3 minutes. Garnish with onion brushes. Serve hot. Makes 4 servings.

Eggplant & Tomato Pizza

1 recipe Traditional Pizza Dough, shaped
  and ready for topping, page 8

Eggplant Topping:
1 pound eggplants
1 garlic clove, crushed
3 tablespoons lemon juice
3 tablespoons chopped fresh parsley
2 green onions, chopped
Salt and pepper

To Finish:
1 pound tomatoes, sliced
1 tablespoon olive oil
2 tablespoons chopped fresh parsley
2 tablespoons freshly grated Parmesan
  cheese
Parsley sprigs, to garnish

First make Eggplant Topping. Preheat
oven to 350F (175C). Put eggplants on
a baking sheet and bake 30 minutes
until soft. Cool. Halve and scoop out
soft centers into a bowl. Add garlic,
lemon juice, parsley and green onions.
Season to taste with salt and pepper.

Increase oven temperature to 425F
(220C). Spread Eggplant Topping over
dough. Arrange sliced tomatoes on top,
brush with oil and season to taste with
salt and pepper. Sprinkle with chopped
parsley and Parmesan cheese. Bake 20
minutes until crust is golden. Garnish
with parsley sprigs. Makes 4 servings.

Note: Eggplant Topping may be made
in advance and refrigerated for 3 to 4
days. It is also delicious served as a dip
with hot toast or pita bread.

Nutty Vegetable Pizza

1 recipe Quick Pizza Dough, shaped and
  ready for topping, page 11
1/3 cup (2 oz.) chopped roasted peanuts

Topping:
1/4 small white cabbage
2 carrots
2 celery stalks
2 tablespoons French dressing
Salt and pepper
4 ounces feta cheese, cubed
Peanut and celery leaves, to garnish

Preheat oven to 425F (220C). Sprinkle
dough with the chopped peanuts and
press in lightly. Bake 15 minutes.

Meanwhile, shred cabbage, grate carrots and slice celery thinly. Place vegetables in a bowl. Add the French dressing and season to taste with salt and
pepper.

Spoon vegetables over the pizza. Arrange cubes of cheese on top. Return to
oven and bake 10 minutes. Garnish
with peanuts and celery leaves. Serve at
once. Makes 4 servings.

Pesto & Mushroom Pizza

1 recipe Pan Pizza Dough, shaped and
 ready for topping, page 10

Pesto Topping:
1 large bunch fresh basil leaves
3 garlic cloves, peeled
1/3 cup (2 oz.) pine nuts
3 tablespoons freshly grated Parmesan
 cheese
Salt and pepper
2/3 cup olive oil
Boiling water

To Finish:
6 ounces button mushrooms, sliced
Olive oil
2/3 cup (3 oz.) mozzarella cheese
2/3 cup (2 oz.) freshly grated Parmesan
 cheese
Basil sprigs and pine nuts, to garnish

Preheat oven to 425F (220C). Make
Topping. In a blender or food processor, process basil leaves, garlic, pine
nuts and 3 tablespoons Parmesan
cheese until chopped. Season to taste
with salt and pepper. With motor run-
ning, add oil in a gentle stream; process
until absorbed. Blend until smooth,
adding a little boiling water if necessary, for a spreading consistency.

Spread topping over dough. Arrange
mushrooms on top; brush with olive oil.
Sprinkle with mozzarella cheese and
Parmesan cheese. Bake 20 minutes until crust is golden. Garnish with basil
sprigs and pine nuts. Makes 4 servings.

Note: Pesto can be made in advance
and stored in a tightly covered jar in the
refrigerator up to 6 days. Ready-made
pesto may be bought in delicatessens
and specialty food shops.

Tapenade & Pepper Pizza

1 recipe Pan Pizza Dough, shaped and
 ready for topping, page 10

Tapenade Topping:
5 ounces pitted green olives
1 (2 oz.) can anchovy fillets
1 (2 oz.) canned tuna in oil, drained
1 oz. capers
1 garlic clove
1 teaspoon Dijon-style mustard
Olive oil
Salt and pepper
Lemon juice

To Finish:
1 green bell pepper, peeled, page 16
1 yellow bell pepper, peeled, page 16
Mint sprigs and a few capers, to garnish

Preheat oven to 425F (220C). Make the
topping. In a blender or food processor, process the olives, anchovy fillets
and oil, tuna, capers, garlic and mustard. Process to a rough-textured
puree. Add a little extra oil if necessary.
Season with salt and pepper and lemon
juice.

Cut bell peppers into strips and then
into diamond shapes. Spread tapenade
over dough. Arrange bell peppers
attractively on top. Drizzle a little more
oil over and season with pepper. Bake
20 minutes until crust is golden. Garnish with mint sprigs and capers. Makes
4 servings.

French Bread Pizza

1 medium French bread loaf
2 tablespoons olive oil
1 (16-oz.) can tomatoes
Salt and pepper
1 (6-oz.) can tuna in oil, drained
8 pimento-stuffed olives
1 cup (4 oz.) shredded Edam cheese
3 green onions, chopped

To Serve:
Green salad

Preheat oven to 350F (175C). Cut a slice from the top of French loaf along the whole length. Scoop out most of the soft crumb from bottom portion (this and the lid will not be required but can be used for bread crumbs).

Brush inside of loaf with half the oil. Drain tomatoes and reserve juice. Brush inside of loaf with juice. Place loaf on a baking sheet and bake 10 minutes.

Chop drained tomatoes and arrange half inside the loaf. Season to taste with salt and pepper. Flake tuna and spoon over tomatoes. Top with remaining tomatoes and season again with salt and pepper.

Halve olives and arrange on top. Sprinkle with cheese. Return to oven and bake 15 minutes. Sprinkle with chopped green onions and serve at once with salad. Makes 2 servings.

Cheese & Onion Pizzas

8 small pita breads

Cheese Topping:
2 tablespoons butter or margarine
2 tablespoons all-purpose flour
2 cups (8 oz.) shredded Cheddar cheese
1/3 cup milk
1 egg yolk
Pinch of dry mustard
Pinch of red (cayenne) pepper

To Finish:
3 green onions, chopped
2 eggs, hard-cooked, chopped
Hard-boiled egg slices and chives, to garnish

Preheat oven to 425F (220C). Make the topping. In a small saucepan, melt butter or margarine. Add flour and cook, stirring, until smooth. Stir in half the cheese, then half the milk. Repeat with remaining cheese and milk. Beat in egg yolk. Stir in mustard and pepper and mix well.

Grease a baking sheet. Place pita breads on greased baking sheet. Spread topping over them. Bake 10 minutes. In a small bowl, mix chopped green onions and chopped hard-cooked eggs together. Sprinkle the mixture over the pizzas and bake 2 minutes. Garnish each pizza with a hard-cooked egg slice and chives. Serve hot. Makes 4 servings.

Creamy Salmon Pizza

1 recipe Whole-Wheat Pizza Dough,
  shaped and ready for topping, page 8

Topping:
1 (16-oz.) can red salmon
1 zucchini, finely chopped
3 tablespoons whipping cream
Salt and pepper
1 teaspoon grated lemon peel
1 tablespoon chopped fresh dill
Olive oil
1/4 cup (3/4 oz.) grated Parmesan cheese
Lemon peel and dill sprigs, to garnish

Preheat oven to 425F (220C). Make the
topping. Drain salmon and discard
bones. Put in a medium bowl and flake
with a fork. Stir in zucchini, cream, salt
and pepper to taste, lemon peel and
dill.

Brush dough with olive oil. Spoon the
salmon mixture on top. Sprinkle with
the Parmesan cheese. Bake 20 minutes
until crust is golden. Garnish with
lemon peel and dill sprigs. Serve at
once. Makes 4 servings.

Cheesy Seafood Pizza

1 recipe Traditional Pizza Dough, shaped
  and ready for topping, page 8

Topping:
1 recipe Cheese Topping, page 20
1 (6-oz.) can tuna, packed in water
6 ounces peeled small shrimp, thawed if
  frozen
1/4 teaspoon **paprika**
Salt and pepper
Lemon twists, coriander sprigs and peeled
  shrimp, to garnish

Preheat oven to 425F (220C). Spread
the Cheese Topping over the pizza
dough.

Drain tuna, put in a bowl and flake
roughly with a fork. Mix in shrimp and
paprika and season to taste with salt
and pepper. Spread mixture over the
Cheese Topping.

Bake 20 minutes until crust is crisp and
golden. Garnish with lemon twists,
coriander sprigs and peeled shrimp.
Makes 4 servings.

Frittata Pizza

1 recipe Traditional Pizza Dough, made up
   to end of Step 2, page 8

Topping:
2 tablespoons olive oil
1 onion, thinly sliced
3 new potatoes, cooked, sliced
8 slices pepper salami
1 small green bell pepper, sliced
8 pitted ripe olives, halved
2 ounces feta cheese, cubed
1 tablespoon chopped fresh parsley
4 cherry tomatoes, halved
6 eggs
Salt and pepper
Watercress to garnish

Preheat oven to 425F (220C). Grease a
deep 10-inch pizza pan or cake pan.
Punch down risen dough and knead
briefly, then press dough into pan.

Brush dough with a little of the oil.
Arrange sliced onion over the top.
Sprinkle with remaining oil. Bake 10
minutes.

Remove pizza from oven. Arrange
sliced potatoes, salami, bell pepper,
olives and cheese over the surface. Add
parsley and tomatoes. In a bowl, beat
together eggs and season to taste with
salt and pepper. Pour over pizza and
bake for 10 to 15 minutes until topping
is puffed and golden. Garnish with
watercress. Makes 4 servings.

Avocado & Crab Bites

1 recipe Traditional Pizza Dough, made up
   to end of step 2, page 8

Topping:
2 avocados
1 tablespoon lemon juice
1/4 cup butter
1/2 cup all-purpose flour
1-1/4 cups milk
Salt and pepper
1/4 teaspoon red (cayenne) pepper
12 ounces crabmeat, thawed if frozen,
   drained
1/2 cup (2 oz.) shredded Gruyère cheese
Avocado slices and tomato, to garnish

Preheat oven to 425F (220C). Punch
down dough and knead briefly. Roll
out dough and use to line a 14" x 10"
jellyroll pan.

Make topping. Halve avocados; remove stones. Scoop out flesh and chop
coarsely. Place in a bowl with lemon
juice and stir lightly to coat. Set aside.

Melt butter in a saucepan. Stir in flour
and cook for 2 minutes. Stir in milk;
bring to a boil. Reduce heat; simmer 2
minutes. Season to taste with salt and
pepper and cayenne.

Remove pan from heat. Stir in crab,
cheese, and chopped avocado. Spread
over the dough, then bake 20 minutes
until crust is golden. Cool slightly before cutting into fingers or squares.
Garnish with avocado slices and tomato. Makes 6 to 8 servings.

Ham & Tomato Bites

1 recipe Traditional Pizza Dough, made to
    end of step 2, page 8

Topping:
1 recipe Tomato Topping, page 12
12 to 14 slices prosciutto
6 ounces mozzarella cheese, sliced
Olives, anchovies and thyme sprigs, to
    garnish.

Preheat oven to 425F (220C). Grease
several baking sheets. Roll out dough
very thinly and cut out 12 to 14 circles
with a 1-1/2- to 2-inch cutter.

Spread dough with Tomato Topping.
Top each circle with a ham slice and a
mozzarella cheese slice. Bake 10 to 12
minutes until the crust is golden and
the cheese has melted. Garnish with
olives, anchovies and thyme. Serve at
once. Makes 6 to 8 servings.

Pesto Pizzelle

1 recipe Traditional Pizza Dough, made to
    end of step 2, page 8

Topping:
6 ounces ricotta cheese
3 tablespoons Pesto Topping, page 19
1 egg, beaten
Basil sprigs, ripe olives and pine nuts, to
    garnish

Preheat oven to 425F (220C). Punch
down dough and knead briefly. Roll
out dough and use to line a 14" x 10"
jellyroll pan.

Make the topping. Beat together ricotta
cheese and Pesto Topping and egg to
make a smooth, firm mixture.

Spread over the dough, then bake 20
minutes until crust is golden. Cool
slightly, then cut into squares or trian-
gles. Garnish with basil, olives and pine
nuts. Serve as a cocktail snack. Makes
10 to 15 servings.

Fresh Herb Pizza

1 recipe Quick Pizza Dough, shaped and ready for topping, page 11

Topping:
2 tablespoons olive oil
1 tablespoon chopped fresh basil
1 tablespoon chopped fresh parsley
1 teaspoon chopped fresh oregano
1-1/2 cups (6 oz.) shredded mozzarella cheese
3/4 cup (2-1/4 oz.) grated Pecorino cheese
Salt and pepper
Fresh herbs, to garnish

Preheat oven to 425F (220C). Brush the dough with 1 tablespoon oil. Sprinkle with chopped herbs. Cover with the cheese and season to taste with salt and pepper. Drizzle with remaining oil. Bake 20 minutes until golden. Garnish with herbs. Makes 4 servings.

Asparagus Ham Squares

1 recipe Traditional Pizza Dough, made up to end of step 2, page 8
1 tablespoon vegetable oil

Topping:
6 ounces sliced ham
6 ounces ricotta cheese
2 tablespoons milk
1 (10-oz.) package frozen asparagus spears thawed
Salt and pepper
Freshly grated Parmesan cheese

Preheat oven to 425F (220C). Grease a 14" x 10" jellyroll pan. Punch down dough and knead briefly. Roll out dough on a lightly floured surface and use to line bottom and sides of pan. Prick bottom with a fork. Brush with oil. Bake 15 minutes until crisp and golden.

Meanwhile, finely chop 4 ounces ham. In a medium bowl, combine chopped ham, cheese and milk. Cut tips from asparagus and reserve. Chop stalks and stir into cheese mixture.

Remove pizza from oven and cool slightly. Spread cheese mixture over dough. Slice remaining ham in strips and arrange in a lattice pattern over dough. Dot asparagus tips on surface, season to taste with salt and pepper and sprinkle with Parmesan cheese. Return to oven and cook 2 minutes. Slide pizza from pan onto a chopping board. With a sharp knife cut off crusts and discard. Cut pizza into small squares or fingers and serve as a cocktail snack. Makes 8 to 10 servings.

Ratatouille & Shrimp Pizza

1 recipe Whole-Wheat Pizza Dough,
   shaped and ready for topping, page 8
1 tablespoon vegetable oil

Topping:
2 tablespoons vegetable oil
1 large onion, chopped
2 garlic cloves, crushed
3 small zucchini, halved
1 small red bell pepper
1 small green bell pepper
1 small yellow bell pepper
8 ounces eggplant, cubed
1 (16-oz.) can tomatoes
2 tablespoons tomato paste
Salt and pepper
4 ounces peeled shrimp, thawed if frozen
Chopped parsley, to garnish

Make the topping. Heat oil in a large saucepan. Add onion and garlic. Cook 3 minutes, stirring. Do not burn garlic.

Cut zucchini and bell peppers into 1/2-inch pieces. Add to pan with eggplant. Drain juice from tomatoes; reserve. Add chopped tomatoes and juice, tomato paste and season to taste with salt and pepper. Stir well and cook 15 minutes until vegetables are cooked and the sauce thickened.

Preheat oven to 425F (220C). Prick dough with a fork and brush with oil. Bake 15 minutes. Stir shrimp into vegetables and spoon on top of crust. Bake 5 minutes. Serve at once sprinkled with parsley. Makes 4 servings.

Mixed Seafood Pizza

1 recipe Traditional Pizza Dough, shaped
   and ready for topping, page 8

Topping:
8 ounces mussels in the shell
2 tablespoons olive oil
2 garlic cloves, crushed
4 ounces squid, cleaned
1 (16-oz.) can chopped tomatoes
Salt and pepper
4 ounces shrimp, cooked, peeled, thawed if
   frozen
8 ounces clean shelled clams or 1 (14-oz.)
   can clams, drained
2 tablespoons chopped fresh parsley
Flat-leaf parsley and lemon, to garnish

Make topping. Scrub mussels and remove beards. Place in a large saucepan with 2 tablespoons water. Cover and cook over medium heat, shaking pan, until all the shells are open.

Strain pan juice and reserve. In a saucepan, heat 1 tablespoon oil and garlic. Slice squid and add to pan. Cook 5 minutes, stirring. Remove squid with a slotted spoon and reserve. Discard garlic. Add tomatoes, reserved mussel juice and season to taste with salt and pepper. Cook gently 30 minutes.

Preheat oven to 425F (220C). Brush dough with remaining oil; prick with a fork. Bake 15 to 20 minutes until golden. Add shrimp and clams to sauce. Cook 10 minutes. Stir in squid and mussels. Remove pizza from oven. Spoon sauce over crust, sprinkle with parsley and return to oven for 10 minutes. Garnish with parsley and lemon, serve at once. Makes 4 servings.

Pizza Canapés

1 recipe Cornmeal Pizza Dough, made up to
   step 2, page 8
1 tablespoon olive oil

Topping:
1 recipe Cheese Topping, page 20
Selection of the following: anchovy fillets,
   stuffed and plain; olives; capers;
   lumpfish roe; cooked shrimp; smoked
   salmon; crisp bacon; smoked quail eggs;
   sprigs of fresh herbs

Preheat oven to 425F (220C). Grease
several baking sheets. Punch down
dough and knead briefly. Roll out
dough very thinly and cut out 10 to 12
small circles with a 1-1/2- to 2-inch cutter. Spread with a little Cheese Topping and arrange on baking sheets.
Bake in the oven 10 to 15 minutes until
golden. Top with desired toppings and
serve at once. Makes 10 to 12 servings.

Mozzolive Bites

1 recipe Cornmeal Pizza Dough, made up to
   end of step 2, page 8

Topping:
4 tablespoons olive oil
6 ounces mozzarella cheese
1 (5-1/2-oz.) jar olive paste
Salt and pepper
Sage leaves and pimento, to garnish

Preheat to 425F (220C). Grease
several baking sheets. Punch down
dough and knead briefly. Roll out
dough and cut as for Pizza Canapés,
see left. Brush with 1 tablespoon oil
and bake 15 to 20 minutes until
golden.

Cut cheese into tiny pieces and place in
a medium bowl. Stir in the olive paste.
Season to taste with salt and pepper.
Spoon a little of the mixture onto each
circle, dividing it equally among them.

Drizzle with remaining oil. Bake 3 to 4
minutes until cheese melts. Garnish
with sage leaves and pimento. Serve at
once as a cocktail snack. Makes 10 to 12
servings.

Artichoke & Cheese Pizza

1 recipe Traditional Pizza Dough, shaped
and ready for topping, page 8

Topping:
3 tablespoons olive oil
1 (14-oz.) can artichoke hearts
Salt and pepper
2 cups (8 oz.) shredded Emmental cheese
Marjoram leaves and sliced pimento, to
garnish

Preheat oven to 425F (220C). Brush the
pizza dough with 1 tablespoon of the
oil.

Drain artichokes and slice thinly. Arrange artichoke slices over dough.
Sprinkle with remaining oil; season to
taste with salt and pepper. Sprinkle the
cheese over the top.

Bake 20 minutes until crust is crisp and
golden and cheese has melted. Garnish
with marjoram leaves and sliced pimento. Serve at once. Makes 4 servings.

Three Salami Pizza

1 recipe Quick Pizza Dough, shaped and
ready for topping, page 15

Topping:
1 tablespoon vegetable oil
3 tomatoes, finely chopped
Salt and pepper
6 ounces mixed sliced salami
1/2 cup (2 oz.) shredded Cheddar cheese
Gherkins, to garnish

Preheat oven to 425F (220C). Brush
dough with the oil.

Spread tomatoes over dough. Season to
taste with salt and pepper. Cut salami
into strips and arrange over tomatoes.
Sprinkle with cheese. Bake 20 minutes
until dough is golden and cheese
melted. Garnish with gherkins. Makes
4 servings.

Mushroom & Cheese Pizza

1 recipe Whole-Wheat Pizza Dough, shaped and ready for topping, page 8

Topping:
1 to 2 tablespoons Dijon-style mustard or 2 tablespoons butter or margarine, melted
4 ounces sliced ham
4 ounces mushrooms, sliced
6 tablespoons sieved tomatoes
1 cup (4 oz.) shredded Cheddar cheese
Salt and pepper
Watercress sprigs, to garnish

Preheat oven to 425F (220C). Spread dough with the mustard, if using, or brush with the melted butter or margarine.

Slice the ham diagonally to form diamond shapes. Arrange over dough. Place one-third of the mushrooms in the center and the remainder in groups around the edge of the pizza. Spoon a little tomato over mushrooms. Sprinkle with cheese. Season to taste with salt and pepper. Bake 20 minutes until crust is crisp and golden and the cheese bubbling. Garnish with watercress. Makes 6 servings.

BLT Pizza

1 recipe Traditional Pizza Dough, shaped and ready for topping, page 8

Filling:
8 bacon slices, crisp-cooked
4 tomatoes, coarsely chopped
1/2 small iceberg lettuce head
4 to 6 tablespoons mayonnaise
Salt and pepper
Shredded lettuce, to garnish

Preheat oven to 425F (220C). With kitchen scissors, cut bacon into pieces. Very finely shred the lettuce. In a bowl, mix bacon, tomatoes, lettuce and mayonnaise and season to taste with salt and pepper.

Spread the mixture over the dough. Bake 20 minutes. Garnish with additional shredded lettuce. Serve at once. Makes 4 servings.

Ground Beef & Onion Pizza

1 recipe Potato Pizza Dough, shaped and
  ready for topping, page 9

Topping:
8 ounces lean ground beef
Salt and pepper
2 tablespoons tomato paste
2 tablespoons Worcestershire sauce
2 tablespoons vegetable oil
4 ounces mushrooms, sliced
1 green bell pepper, sliced in rings
1 small onion, sliced crosswise
Watercress, chives and red bell pepper, to
  garnish

Make the topping. In a medium saucepan, cook the beef until browned; drain
off any fat. Season to taste with salt and
pepper. Add tomato paste and Worcestershire sauce. Cook 15 minutes, stirring the mixture occasionally.

Preheat oven to 425F (220C). Brush
dough with 1 tablespoon oil. Arrange
mushrooms on dough. Spoon meat
mixture on top. Arrange rings of bell
pepper and onion over meat mixture
and brush with remaining oil. Bake 20
minutes until crust is crisp and golden.
Garnish with watercress bunches tied
with chives and red bell pepper. Makes
4 servings.

Sardine & Tomato Pizza

1 recipe Traditional Pizza Dough, shaped
  and ready for topping, page 8

Topping:
4 tablespoons tomato sauce
1 (4 oz.) can sardines in oil, drained
2 tomatoes, sliced
4 processed cheese slices
Cress sprouts, to garnish

Preheat oven to 425F (220C). Spread
tomato sauce over the dough. Split sardines horizontally and arrange around
the edge. Make a circle of overlapping
tomatoes in the center.

Cut cheese strips and arrange in a lattice over the tomatoes. Bake 20 minutes
until the crust is golden. Garnish with
sprouts. Serve hot. Makes 6 servings.

Bolognese Pizza

1 recipe Potato Pizza Dough, with
   Parmesan cheese, shaped and ready for
   topping, page 9

Topping:
2 tablespoons vegetable oil
3 bacon slices, chopped
1 onion, finely chopped
1 carrot, finely chopped
1 stalk celery, finely chopped
1 garlic clove, crushed
8 ounces lean ground beef
1 tablespoon tomato paste
1/4 teaspoon Italian seasoning
1/2 cup beef stock
Salt and pepper

To Serve:
Freshly grated Parmesan cheese
Tomato and marjoram sprigs, to garnish

Make the topping. In a medium saucepan, heat oil; add bacon. Cook 2 minutes. Add onion, carrot, celery and garlic. Cook, stirring, until soft. Add
ground beef and cook, stirring until
brown. Drain off fat.

Stir in tomato paste, Italian seasoning
and stock; season to taste with salt and
pepper. Cover and simmer 30 minutes.

Preheat oven to 425F (220C). Spoon
sauce on top of dough. Bake 20 minutes until crust is crisp and golden.
Sprinkle with Parmesan cheese and
garnish with tomato and marjoram.
Makes 6 servings.

Tuna & Onion Pizza

1 recipe Pan Pizza Dough, shaped and
   ready for topping, page 10

Topping:
2 tablespoons vegetable oil
1 (16-oz.) can chopped tomatoes
1 bunch green onions, chopped
1 (7-oz) can tuna, drained
Salt and pepper

Preheat oven to 425F (220C). Brush
dough with 1 tablespoon oil. Bake 20
minutes until golden.

Make the topping. Drain tomatoes,
reserving juice. Chop tomatoes. In a
medium saucepan, heat the chopped
tomatoes and remaining oil. Add half
the onions to pan; cook 10 minutes.
Flake tuna; stir into tomato mixture.
Season to taste with salt and pepper.

Spoon onto dough and bake in the oven
3 to 5 minutes. Shred remaining
onions; sprinkle over pizza to serve.
Makes 6 servings.

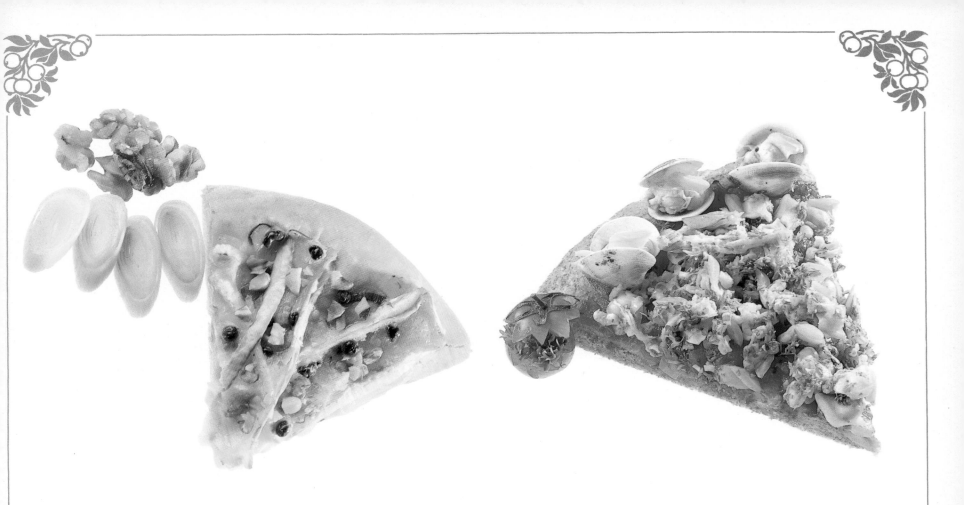

French Brie Pizza

1 recipe Traditional Pizza Dough, with
    walnuts, shaped and ready for topping,
    page 8

Topping:
2 small leeks, finely shredded
2 tablespoons walnut or olive oil
Salt
8 ounces Brie or Camembert cheese, thinly
    sliced
1 teaspoon green peppercorns, drained
2 tablespoons chopped walnuts

Preheat oven to 425F (220C). Make the
topping. Put leeks in a medium saucepan with 1 tablespoon oil. Cook gently
5 minutes, stirring, until soft. Brush
dough with remaining oil, then top
with leeks. Season to taste with salt.

Arrange cheese over leeks. Lightly
crush some or all of the peppercorns
and sprinkle over leeks. Scatter walnuts
over top. Bake 20 minutes until crust is
crisp and golden. Makes 4 servings.

Pizza with Clams

1 recipe Whole-Wheat Pizza Dough,
    shaped and ready for topping, page 8

Topping:
1 pound clams in the shell or 1 (14-oz.) can
    clams
3 tablespoons olive oil
1 recipe Tomato Topping, page 12
Salt and pepper
Few drops hot pepper sauce
2 tablespoons chopped fresh parsley

Preheat oven to 425F (220C). If using
clams in the shell, wash well and place
in a saucepan with 1 tablespoon oil.
Cover and cook over low heat until all
the shells open. Discard any that do not
open. Remove from heat; strain pan
juices into a bowl. Reserve. Remove
clams from their shells, reserving a few
intact for garnishing. Place shelled
clams in reserved juice.

Spread Tomato Topping over dough.
Drizzle with remaining oil. Season to
taste with salt and pepper and hot pepper sauce and 1 tablespoon chopped
parsley. Bake 20 minutes until crust is
crisp and golden. Spoon the shelled
clams (or canned clams) and a little
clam juice over pizza. Arrange reserved
clams in shells on top. Sprinkle with
remaining chopped parsley. Makes 4
servings.

Mexican Chile Pizza

1 recipe Cornmeal Pizza Dough, made up to
   end of step 2, page 8

Topping:
1 pound lean ground beef
1 onion, chopped
1 garlic clove, crushed
Salt and pepper
1 teaspoon ground cumin
1 teaspoon chile powder
2 teaspoons tomato paste
1 (15-oz.) can kidney beans, drained
3 tomatoes, chopped
1 (7-oz.) can whole-kernel corn, drained
1 green bell pepper, chopped
4 to 6 green onions, chopped
1/2 cup (2 oz.) shredded Cheddar cheese

Guacamole:
2 ripe avocados
Juice of 1 lemon
Salt and pepper
3 green onions
Few drops hot pepper sauce

Preheat oven to 425F (220C). Grease a
14" x 10" jellyroll pan. Punch down
dough; knead briefly and place in center of pan. Press out to sides; pinch up
edges to create a rim.

In a medium saucepan, cook beef, onion and garlic until meat browns, stirring to break up meat. Drain off fat.
Season with salt and pepper. Add spices
and tomato paste. Cook 10 minutes.

Rinse and mash kidney beans. Spread
beans over dough. Spoon meat mixture
on top.

Arrange tomatoes, corn and bell pepper and onions on top of pizza as shown
in photo. Sprinkle with cheese. Bake 20
minutes until crust is golden. Make
guacamole by mixing all ingredients in
a blender until smooth. Serve with pizza. Makes 6 to 8 servings.

Pissaladière

1 recipe Traditional Pizza Dough, shaped
   and ready for topping, page 8

Topping:
1 (16-oz.) can tomatoes
1 onion, chopped
1 garlic clove, crushed
2 tablespoons olive oil
1 tablespoon chopped fresh parsley
2 teaspoons chopped fresh thyme or
   1 teaspoon dried thyme
1 tablespoon tomato paste
1 egg
1/2 cup (2 oz.) shredded Gruyère cheese
Salt and pepper
1 (2-oz.) can anchovy fillets
Ripe olives

Make the topping. Drain tomatoes,
reserving juice. Finely chop tomatoes.
In a saucepan, heat chopped tomatoes
and their juice, onion, garlic, 1 tablespoon oil, parsley, thyme and tomato
paste together. Bring to a boil. Reduce
heat; simmer 30 minutes. Cool slightly.

Preheat oven to 425F (220C). Brush
dough with remaining oil.

Beat egg and stir into tomato mixture
with cheese. Spread over dough. Season to taste with salt and pepper. Drain
and cut anchovy fillets in thin strips.
Arrange in a lattice over pizza. Place
olives in centers of lattice. Bake 20 minutes until crust is crisp and golden.
Makes 4 servings.

Spanish Pizza

1 recipe Traditional Pizza Dough, shaped
  and ready for topping, page 8

Topping:
3 skinned, boneless chicken breasts,
  cooked
1 tablespoon olive oil
1 onion, chopped
2 bacon slices, chopped
1-1/4 cups long-grain rice
1/2 cup dry white wine
1/2 cup chicken stock
Salt and pepper
1 red bell pepper, chopped
4 ounces chorizo or garlic sausage, sliced
4 tomatoes, seeded, chopped
Few strands saffron, if desired
Parsley and chopped bell pepper, to
  garnish

Make the topping. Cut the chicken into
cubes and set aside. In a medium saucepan, heat oil; add the onion and bacon
and fry 5 minutes. Add rice, wine, and
stock. Season with salt and pepper.
Bring to a boil, cover and cook 5 minutes.

Stir in chopped bell pepper, chorizo or
garlic sausage, tomatoes and saffron, if
desired. Reduce heat, then simmer 12
to 15 minutes until rice is tender and
most of the liquid has reduced. Stir in
chicken.

Meanwhile, preheat oven to 425F
(220C). Spoon topping on top of the
dough, then bake 20 minutes. Garnish
with parsley and bell pepper. Makes 6
servings.

Swiss Cheese Pizza

1 recipe Traditional Pizza Dough, shaped
  and ready for topping, page 8
1 tablespoon vegetable oil

Topping:
1 garlic clove, chopped
1-1/2 cups (6 oz.) Cheddar cheese
1-1/2 cups (6 oz.) shredded Gruyère cheese
2 tablespoons kirsch
Freshly grated nutmeg
Pepper
Pimento strips and oregano sprigs, to
  garnish

Preheat oven to 425F (220C). Sprinkle
dough with garlic and shredded cheese.
Sprinkle with kirsch, nutmeg and pepper. Bake 20 minutes until crust is crisp
and golden.

Garnish the pizza with pimento and
oregano. Makes 6 to 8 servings.

Variation: Substitute Emmentaler
cheese for the Gruyère cheese, if preferred.

Mushroom Calzone

1 recipe Traditional Pizza Dough, made to
end of step 2, page 8

Filling:
1 pound mushrooms, sliced
2 tablespoons olive oil
1 garlic clove, sliced
Salt and pepper
1/2 teaspoon dried leaf oregano
8 ounces ricotta cheese
2 tablespoons freshly grated Parmesan
cheese
Beaten egg, to glaze
Grated Parmesan cheese and oregano
sprigs, to garnish

Make the filling. In a medium saucepan, heat oil. Add mushrooms and
garlic; cook 3 to 4 minutes. Remove
with a slotted spoon and place in a bowl.
Season to taste with salt and pepper;
add oregano. Mix in ricotta cheese and
2 tablespoons Parmesan cheese.

Preheat oven to 425F (220C). Grease 2
baking sheets. Divide dough into 2
equal pieces. Roll out each piece on a
lightly floured surface to a 10-inch circle. Brush lightly with oil.

Divide filling between the 2 dough
pieces, confining it to one half of each
circle. Dampen edges with water, then
fold dough over to enclose filling and
seal well by pressing with a fork. Transfer to baking sheets, brush with beaten
egg and make 2 or 3 air holes with a
sharp knife. Bake 20 minutes until
golden. Garnish with grated Parmesan
cheese and oregano sprigs. Makes 4 to 6
servings.

Leek & Onion Calzone

1 recipe Traditional Pizza Dough, made to
end of step 2, page 8

Filling:
3 tablespoons olive oil
2 small leeks, sliced
2 onions, sliced
1 large Spanish onion, sliced
1/2 cup dry white wine
1/2 cup half and half
Salt and pepper
Freshly grated nutmeg
4 ounces stuffed olives, chopped
1 tablespoon olive oil
Leek, onion and olive halves, to garnish

In a medium saucepan, heat 3 tablespoons oil over low heat. Add leeks and
onions; cook 10 minutes until soft. Increase heat, add wine and cook until
almost dry.

Reduce heat; add half and half. Season
to taste with salt, pepper and nutmeg.
Cook 2 to 3 minutes until creamy. Remove from heat, stir in chopped olives
and set aside.

Preheat oven to 425F (220C). Grease 2
baking sheets. Divide dough into 2
equal pieces. Roll out each piece on a
lightly floured surface to a 10-inch circle. Brush lightly with 1 tablespoon oil.

Divide filling between the 2 dough
pieces, confining it to one half of each
circle. Dampen edges with water, then
fold dough over to enclose filling and
seal well by pressing with a fork. Transfer to baking sheets, brush with beaten
egg and make 2 or 3 air holes with a
sharp knife. Bake 20 minutes until
golden. Garnish with leek, onion and
olive slices. Makes 4 to 6 servings.

Chicken Liver Calzone

1 recipe Traditional Pizza Dough, made to
   end of step 2, page 8

Filling:
1/4 cup butter
1 pound chicken livers, trimmed
6 bacon slices, chopped
1 tablespoon chopped fresh sage
1-1/2 pounds fresh spinach, trimmed
Salt and pepper
Lemon juice
Freshly grated nutmeg
Beaten egg, to glaze
Sage leaves, to garnish

Make the filling. In a medium saucepan, melt butter. Add livers; cook
quickly until brown but still pink on the
inside. Remove with slotted spoon and
serve.

Add bacon to saucepan; cook until
crisp. Remove with slotted spoon and
add to livers with chopped sage. Add
spinach to saucepan. Cover and cook
until wilted. Drain well, then chop
coarsely. Season to taste with salt and
pepper, lemon juice and nutmeg.

Preheat oven to 425 (220C). Grease 2
baking sheets. Divide dough into 2
equal pieces. Roll out both pieces on a
lightly floured surface to 10-inch circles. Brush lightly with oil.

Divide filling between the 2 dough
pieces, confining it to one half of each
circle. Dampen edges with water, then
fold dough over to enclose filling and
seal well by pressing with a fork. Transfer to baking sheets, brush with beaten
egg and make 2 or 3 air holes with a
sharp knife. Bake 20 minutes until
golden. Makes 4 to 6 servings.

Broccoli Calzone

1 recipe Pan Pizza Dough, made up to end
   of step 1, page 10
1 teaspoon dried dill weed
1 tablespoon olive oil

Filling:
12 ounces broccoli
2 cups (8 oz.) shredded Cheddar cheese
Salt and pepper
Beaten egg, to glaze
Chopped fresh dill, to garnish

In a medium saucepan of boiling water,
blanch broccoli 2 minutes. Drain and
refresh with cold water. Drain again.
Chop coarsely.

Preheat oven to 425F (220C). Grease 2
baking sheets. Knead dough with dill
weed until evenly distributed. Divide
into 2 equal pieces. Roll out each piece
on a lightly floured surface to a 10-inch
circle. Brush lightly with oil.

Divide broccoli between the 2 dough
pieces, confining it to one half of each
circle. Sprinkle with two-thirds of the
cheese and season with salt and pepper.
Dampen edges with water, fold dough
over to enclose filling and seal well by
pressing with a fork. Transfer to baking
sheets, brush with beaten egg and
sprinkle with remaining cheese. Make 2
or 3 air holes with a sharp knife. Bake
20 minutes until golden. Garnish with
fresh dill. Makes 4 to 6 servings.

Watercress Pizza Rolls

1 recipe Pan Pizza Dough, made up to end of step 1, page 10

Filling:
2 tablespoons butter
1 onion, finely chopped
3 bunches watercress, finely chopped
8 ounces cottage cheese
3 tablespoons grated Parmesan cheese
1 tablespoon lemon juice
1 egg, beaten
Salt and pepper
Watercress sprigs, to garnish

Make the filling. In a medium saucepan, melt butter. Add onion; cook 5 minutes until soft. Add chopped watercress and cook 3 minutes. Remove from heat, stir in cottage cheese, 2 tablespoons Parmesan cheese, lemon juice and egg. Season to taste with salt and pepper. Cool and chill until firm.

Grease a baking sheet. Roll out dough on a lightly floured surface to a 14" x 10" rectangle.

Spread filling evenly over dough leaving a small border on all sides. Roll up from one long side to make a firm roll. Seal edges well. Cut into 8 to 10 slices and arrange on greased baking sheet. Cover with plastic wrap and let rise for about 30 minutes.

Meanwhile, preheat oven to 425F (220C). Sprinkle with remaining 1 tablespoon Parmesan cheese. Bake 20 minutes until crisp and golden. Garnish with watercress sprigs. Makes 4 to 6 servings.

Pizza Piperade

1 recipe Cornmeal Pizza Dough, made up to end of step 2, page 8

Topping:
6 eggs
Salt and pepper
1 orange bell pepper, halved
1 yellow bell pepper, halved
2 large or 4 small green onions
1 tablespoon olive oil
2 tablespoons chopped fresh parsley
Yellow bell pepper rings and parsley sprigs, to garnish

Preheat oven to 425F (220C). Grease a deep 10-inch pizza pan. Punch down dough and knead briefly on a lightly floured surface. Place dough in center of pan, press out to side.

Beat eggs together in a medium bowl. Season with salt and pepper to taste. Set aside.

Slice bell peppers into strips; cut onions into 1-inch pieces. Heat oil in a medium saucepan, add peppers and onions and cook 3 minutes, stirring constantly. Spoon over dough. Pour egg mixture over bell peppers. Sprinkle with chopped parsley. Bake 20 minutes until the egg mixture is set and golden. Garnish with bell pepper rings and parsley sprigs. Makes 4 servings.

Pizza Ring

1 recipe Traditional Pizza Dough, made up to end of step 2, page 8
1/2 cup (1-1/2 oz.) freshly grated Parmesan cheese
Salt and pepper

Filling:
2-1/2 ounces pepper salami, sliced
1-1/2 ounces smoked cheese
2-1/2 ounces mozzarella cheese
1-1/2 ounces Gruyère cheese
4 slices processed Cheddar cheese
2 hard-cooked eggs
1 tablespoon olive oil
Lettuce leaves and cherry tomatoes, to garnish

Grease a 9-inch ring pan. Punch down dough, then knead dough with Parmesan cheese and salt and pepper to taste. Roll out on a lightly floured surface to a 14" x 10" rectangle.

Chop salami and all the cheese into small pieces. Mix together.

Sprinkle cheese mixture over dough, leaving a narrow border on all sides. Halve eggs and cut each half into 3 pieces. Arrange in lines from top to bottom across the length of dough. Roll up from one long side and seal edges well.

Coil into a circle and seal ends together. Fit into greased ring pan. Cover with plastic wrap and let rise 1 hour until dough is just below top of tin. Brush with oil.

Preheat oven to 425F (220C). Bake 45 minutes until golden. Serve cold. Garnish with lettuce leaves and cherry tomatoes. Makes 6 servings.

Salmon Calzoncelli

1 recipe Traditional Pizza Dough, made up to end of step 2, page 8

Topping:
4 ounces cream cheese, softened
8 ounces thinly sliced smoked salmon
Pepper
Juice of 1/2 lemon
Lemon slices and chives, to garnish

Preheat oven to 425F (220C). Grease 2 baking sheets. Punch down dough and knead briefly. Roll out dough on a lightly floured surface to 1/8 inch thick. Using a 3-inch cutter, cut out as many circles as possible. Keep covered with a towel while re-rolling dough and cutting out more to make a total of 10 to 15.

In a bowl, mix cream cheese and smoked salmon, pepper and lemon juice. Place 1 teaspoon of mixture on one half of each circle. Dampen edges with water, fold over to enclose filling and seal well by pressing with a fork. Transfer to baking sheets and bake 10 to 15 minutes until golden. Garnish with lemon slices and chives. Serve hot or cold. Makes 10 to 15 servings.

Ham & Salami Calzoncelli

1 recipe Traditional Pizza Dough, made up to end of step 2, page 8

Filling:
2 ounces sliced ham
2 ounces sliced salami
2 ounces mozzarella cheese
2 tablespoons chopped fresh parsley
1 tablespoon freshly grated Parmesan cheese
1 egg, beaten
Salt and pepper
Cress sprouts and radish slices, to garnish

Preheat oven to 425F (220C). Grease 2 baking sheets. Punch down dough and knead briefly. Roll out and cut dough as for Salmon Calzoncelli, page 37.

Chop ham and salami very finely. Place in a medium bowl. Shred mozzarella cheese. Add shredded cheese, parsley and parmesan cheese to ham mixture. Stir in egg and season to taste with salt and pepper. Mix thoroughly.

Place 1 teaspoon of the mixture on one half of each circle. Dampen edge with water, then fold over to enclose filling and seal well by pressing with a fork. Transfer to baking sheets and bake 15 minutes until golden. Garnish with cress sprouts and radish slices. Serve hot or cold. Makes 10 to 15 servings.

Variation: Chop 3 ounces mushrooms finely and mix with 6 tablespoons Tomato Topping, page 12, and 1 tablespoon freshly grated Parmesan cheese. Use as the filling.

Leafy Green Calzone

1 recipe Traditional Pizza Dough, made up to end of step 2, page 8

Filling:
1 pound Swiss chard
3 tablespoons olive oil
2 onions, chopped
1 (16-oz.) can tomatoes, drained, chopped
2 garlic cloves
1/2 teaspoon dried leaf oregano
Salt and pepper
Beaten egg, to glaze
Tomato slices and marjoram sprigs, to garnish

Trim and discard hard stalks from Swiss chard. Wash well and cook in a large saucepan (with just the water that clings to the leaves) 10 minutes until tender. Drain well and chop finely.

Heat 2 tablespoons oil in a medium saucepan. Add onions; cook 4 minutes until soft. Add tomatoes, garlic and oregano; season to taste with salt and pepper. Cook 20 minutes until thick.

Preheat oven to 425F (220C). Grease 2 baking sheets. Punch down dough and knead briefly. Divide dough into 2 equal pieces. Roll out each piece on a lightly floured surface to a 10-inch circle. Lightly brush with remaining oil.

Mix tomato mixture with the cooked greens. Divide between the 2 dough pieces, confining mixture to one half of each circle. Dampen edges with water. Fold dough over to cover filling and seal well by pressing with a fork. Place on baking sheets, brush with beaten egg and make 2 or 3 air holes with a sharp knife. Bake 20 minutes until golden. Garnish with tomato and marjoram. Serve hot. Makes 4 servings.

Country Calzone

1 recipe Traditional Pizza Dough, made to end of step 2, page 8
2 tablespoons olive oil
Mushroom slices and thyme sprigs, to garnish

Filling:
1 pound Italian sausages
10 ounces goat's cheese, such as Chèvre
4 ounces mushrooms, sliced
6 to 8 dried tomatoes in oil, see Note
2 dried red chiles, crushed
Beaten egg, to glaze

Preheat oven to 425F (220C). Grease 2 baking sheets. Punch down dough and knead briefly. Divide dough into 2 equal pieces. Roll out each on a lightly floured surface to a 10-inch circle. Brush lightly with oil.

Remove skin from sausages and discard. Cook sausage in a medium skillet, stirring to break up meat. Sprinkle over circles of dough, confining it to one half of circle. Chop cheese coarsely and sprinkle over sausage. Cut dried tomatoes into pieces. Sprinkle tomato pieces, mushrooms and crushed chiles over sausage and cheese.

Fold dough over to enclose filling, dampen edges with water and seal with a fork. Transfer to baking sheets, brush with beaten egg and make 2 or 3 air holes with a sharp knife. Bake 20 minutes until golden. Garnish with mushrooms and thyme. Makes 4 servings.

Note: Dried tomatoes in oil are available from gourmet food shops.

Plum Pizza

1 recipe Deep Pan Pizza Dough, made up to end of Step 1, page 10

Custard Topping:
7 teaspoons cornstarch
4-1/2 teaspoons sugar
1-1/4 cups milk
Few drops vanilla extract
Few drops yellow food coloring, if desired
1-1/2 pounds plums, halved, pitted
2 tablespoons shredded coconut

To Serve:
Whipped cream

Preheat oven to 425F (220C). Grease a deep pizza pan. Place dough in center, press to edge with your knuckles, then cover and let rise until halfway up the pan.

Meanwhile, make topping. In a bowl, blend cornstarch and sugar with a little of the milk until smooth. Heat remaining milk until nearly boiling. Stir into cornstarch mixture, then return to pan. Bring to a boil, stirring until thickened. Remove from heat, stir in vanilla and yellow food coloring, if desired. Let cool a little.

Slice plum halves into sections. Spoon custard on top of dough. Arrange plum slices on top and sprinkle with coconut. Bake 20 minutes. Serve hot or cold with cream. Makes 4 to 6 servings.

Choc-Truffle Pizza

1 recipe Pizza Dough, Page 8

Topping:
1 recipe Custard Topping, page 39
3 ounces baking chocolate, melted
8 ounces sponge cake crumbs
1 tablespoon apricot jam
3 ounces white chocolate, melted
1/2 cup finely chopped almonds
White chocolate curls, to decorate

Preheat oven to 425F (220C). Bake dough 20 minutes until golden. Cool.

Meanwhile, make topping. In a bowl, combine custard and melted dark chocolate. Chill until firm.

Make truffles: combine cake crumbs, jam and white chocolate in a bowl until a stiff paste is formed. Divide mixture into small balls and roll in the chopped almonds to coat.

To assemble pizza, spread chocolate-flavored custard on top of baked crust and arrange truffles around the edge. Sprinkle with white chocolate curls. Makes 6 servings.

Raspberry Mallow Pizza

1 recipe Crumble Pizza Dough, made up to end of step 3, page 10

Topping:
3 tablespoons raspberry jam
1 pound raspberries
6 ounces marshmallows
Few raspberries and raspberry leaves to decorate, if desired

Preheat oven to 425F (220C). Bake pizza dough 5 minutes. Remove from oven, reduce temperature to 350F (175C).

In a small bowl, beat jam until soft. Spread over baked crust. Top with raspberries. Arrange marshmallows over the raspberries. Bake 15 to 20 minutes until marshmallows are soft. Cool before serving. Decorate with raspberries and raspberry leaves, if desired. Makes 6 to 8 servings.

Tropical Pizza

1 recipe Traditional Pizza Dough, shaped
  and ready for topping, page 8

Topping:
8 ounces fresh dates
4 ounces cream cheese, softened
1 small pineapple
2 kiwifruit

Preheat oven to 425F (220C). Prick
dough with a fork, then bake 20 minutes until golden. Cool.

Meanwhile, halve and pit dates. Reserve a few for decoration, then chop
the remainder and put in a bowl with
the cream cheese. Mix well, then set
aside.

Cut top and bottom from pineapple,
then cut off skin. Halve pineapple, slice
thinly and cut out hard central core.
Peel kiwifruit; slice thinly.

Spread cream cheese mixture over
baked crust. Arrange slices of pineapple and kiwifruit on top. Decorate with
reserved date halves. Cover and re-
frigerate until ready to serve. Makes 6
servings.

Berry Streusel Pizza

1 recipe Traditional Pizza Dough, shaped
  and ready for topping, page 8

Topping:
1 cup self-rising flour
1/3 cup sugar
1/3 butter
1 teaspoon ground cinnamon
2 tablespoons water
1 recipe Custard Topping, see page 39
1 (1-lb.) can gooseberries, drained

To Serve:
Whipped cream

Preheat oven to 425F (220C). Prick
dough with a fork and bake 20 minutes
until golden. Cool slightly.

In a medium bowl, mix flour and sugar;
cut in butter until mixture resembles
bread crumbs. Stir in cinnamon and
water; mix with a fork until lumpy.

Spoon custard on top of baked crust,
top with gooseberries, then sprinkle
crumble topping over gooseberries.
Bake 10 to 15 minutes until light gold-
en. Serve hot with whipped cream.
Makes 6 servings.

Cherry & Almond Pizza

1 recipe Traditional Pizza Dough, made up
    to end of step 2, page 8
2 tablespoons ground almonds

Topping:
2 egg whites
3/4 cup ground almonds
1/3 cup sugar
Few drops almond extract
8 ounces Morello cherries in juice
1/2 cup sliced almonds
4 tablespoons Morello cherry jam
Powdered sugar for dusting
Whipped cream, to decorate

Preheat oven to 425F (220C). Punch down dough and knead dough with 2 tablespoons ground almonds.

In a bowl, lightly whisk egg whites. Stir in ground almonds, sugar and almond extract. Spread over dough.

Drain cherries, reserving juice. Spoon over almond mixture, reserving a few for decoration. Sprinkle with sliced almonds; bake 20 minutes until crust is crisp and golden.

Meanwhile, in a saucepan, heat reserved juice and jam until syrupy. Dust cooked pizza with powdered sugar and decorate with whipped cream and reserved cherries. Serve the sauce separately. Makes 6 servings.

Apple Pie Pizza

1 recipe Crumble Pizza Dough, made up to
    end of step 3, page 10

Topping:
3 tablespoons apple or pear butter
2 tablespoons apple juice or water
3 Granny Smith apples, peeled, cored
2 tablespoons raisins
1/2 cup chopped walnuts
1/3 cup packed brown sugar
1 teaspoon ground cinnamon
4 ounces marzipan

To Serve
Apple slices and whipped cream

Preheat oven to 425F (220C). Bake dough 10 minutes. Remove from oven and reduce temperature to 350F (175C).

Mix apple or pear butter with apple juice or water to form a soft paste. Spread over baked crust. Slice apples thinly. Place in a medium bowl with the raisins, walnuts, sugar and cinnamon. Mix well. Spoon over baked crust and level surface. Grate marzipan and sprinkle over surface. Bake 25 to 30 minutes. Serve with apple slices and whipped cream. Makes 6 servings.

Lemon Meringue Pizza

1 recipe Traditional Pizza Dough, shaped
and ready for topping, page 8

Topping:
3 tablespoons cornstarch
1-1/4 cups sugar
1/3 cup water
2 eggs, separated
Juice and grated peel of 2 lemons
Star fruit slices and lemon balm, to garnish

Preheat oven to 425F (220C). Prick dough with a fork. Bake 20 minutes until golden. Cool slightly. Reduce oven temperature to 350F (175C).

Make topping. In a medium saucepan, combine cornstarch and 1 cup sugar. In a small bowl, combine water and egg yolk. Stir egg yolk mixture into sugar mixture. Cook, stirring, over medium heat until bubbly and thickened. Stir in lemon juice and peel. Spread over baked crust.

In a large bowl, whisk egg white until soft peaks form. Whisk in remaining sugar gradually. Pipe or spoon on top of lemon mixture to cover filling completely. Bake 10 minutes until meringue is golden. Decorate with slices of star fruit and lemon balm leaves. Makes 6 servings.

Christmas Calzone

1 recipe Pan Pizza Dough, made up to end
of step 1, page 10

Filling:
1/2 cup unsalted butter, softened
3/4 cup powdered sugar, sifted
2/3 cup packed brown sugar
1 tablespoon milk
1 tablespoon brandy
6 tablespoons mincemeat
Powdered sugar for dusting

Preheat oven to 425F (220C). Grease 2 baking sheets. Divide dough into 2 equal pieces. Roll out each piece to a 10-inch circle.

Make the filling. In a bowl, beat butter and sugars together. Gradually stir in milk and brandy until mixture is light and fluffy.

Place 1 tablespoon brandy butter and 3 tablespoons mincemeat to one side of each circle of dough. Brush edges with water, fold over and seal edges firmly. Transfer to baking sheets and bake 20 minutes until golden.

Dust with powdered sugar. Serve warm with remaining brandy butter. Makes 4 to 6 servings.

Pear & Ginger Pizza

1 recipe Pan Pizza Dough, shaped and ready for topping, page 10

Topping:
4 pears, peeled, cored
3 tablespoons apple or pear butter
1/2 cup chopped walnuts
2 tablespoons chopped crystallized ginger
2 tablespoons butter, melted
Crystallized ginger and angelica, to decorate

Preheat oven to 425F (220C). Chop 2 pears and put in a medium bowl with the apple or pear butter, walnuts and ginger. Mix well, then spread over the dough.

Halve remaining pears. With a sharp knife, slice each half from the round end to the point without cutting through. Fan out the section and arrange on top of the pizza. Brush with melted butter. Bake 20 minutes. Decorate with crystallized ginger and angelica and serve with whipped cream. Makes 4 to 6 servings.

Banana-Maple Syrup Pizza

1 recipe Traditional Pizza Dough, shaped and ready for topping, page 8

Topping:
2 tablespoons butter, melted
4 bananas
2 to 3 tablespoons maple syrup
Chopped walnuts and whipped cream, to decorate

Preheat oven to 425F (220C). Brush dough with a little melted butter.

In a bowl, mash 2 bananas with maple syrup. Spread over dough. Slice remaining bananas. Arrange over mashed bananas. Brush with remaining melted butter. Bake 20 minutes until crust is crisp and brown.

Pipe whipped cream around edge of pizza. Decorate with walnuts. Makes 4 to 6 servings.

Orange Liqueur Pizza

1 recipe Pan Pizza Dough, shaped and
   ready for topping, page 10

Topping:
2 tablespoons butter, melted
3 oranges
2 tablespoons orange liqueur
2 tablespoons orange marmalade
2 tablespoons brown sugar
Whipped cream and mint sprigs, to
   decorate

Preheat oven to 425F (220C). Brush
dough with melted butter.

Using a zester, remove strips of orange
peel; set aside for decoration. Peel
oranges thinly with a sharp knife or
potato peeler. Cut off white pith and
discard. Slice oranges thinly. Arrange
over dough.

In a pan, heat liqueur, marmalade and
sugar until syrupy. Spoon over oranges
and bake 20 minutes. Meanwhile,
blanch peel strips in boiling water 2 to 3
minutes. Drain and cool. Decorate pizza with orange peel strips, cream and
mint. Makes 6 servings.

Berry Cheesecake Pizza

1 recipe Crumble Pizza Dough, made up to
   end of step 3, page 10

Topping:
1-1/2 pints strawberries
12 ounces Neûfchatel cheese
1/2 cup milk
Grated peel of 1/2 orange
1/4 cup orange juice
2 tablespoons honey
1 egg, beaten
2 tablespoons red currant jelly
Whipped cream and strawberry leaves, to
   decorate

Preheat oven to 425F (220C). Bake
dough 15 minutes. Meanwhile, hull
and chop half the strawberries. In a
medium bowl, blend Neûfchatel cheese
with milk, orange peel, orange juice,
honey and egg.

Spoon chopped strawberries over
baked crust. Spoon cheese mixture
over strawberries and smooth top. Bake
35 to 40 minutes until set. Switch off
oven, open door and allow cheesecake
to cool gradually.

In a saucepan, heat red currant jelly
until melted. Arrange reserved
strawberries on top of cheesecake.
Brush with melted jelly. Decorate with
whipped cream. Makes 6 servings.

Panettone

2 (1/4-oz.) packages active dried yeast
1/3 cup warm water (110F, 45C)
1/3 cup sugar
4 egg yolks
1 teaspoon vanilla extract
Grated peel of 1 lemon
3 cups bread flour
1/2 teaspoon salt
1/3 cup butter, softened
1/3 cup chopped candied peel
2 tablespoons dark raisins
2 tablespoons golden raisins
1/4 cup butter, melted

In a small bowl, combine yeast, 1 teaspoon sugar and the water; leave until frothy.

In a large bowl, combine remaining sugar, egg yolks, vanilla and lemon peel. Stir in yeast mixture. Mix flour with salt. Gradually add two-thirds flour to yeast mixture to form a sticky dough.

Divide softened butter into 3 equal pieces. Add one piece at a time, kneading until mixture is heavy and stringy. Add remaining flour; mix well. Knead on a lightly floured surface until firm and buttery, but not sticky. Place in a bowl. Cover with plastic wrap; let rise in a warm place 1-1/2 hours until doubled.

Preheat oven to 400F (205C). Well grease a charlotte pan. Knead peel and raisins into dough. Place in pan, cover and let rise to just below top of pan.

Brush with melted butter; bake 10 minutes. Reduce temperature to 350F (175C). Brush again with butter; bake 30 to 40 minutes until browned. Brush with more butter after 15 minutes. Cool. Makes 10 to 12 servings.

Grape Bread

1 recipe Pizza Dough, made up to end of
  step 1, page 10
2 tablespoons fine sugar

Filling:
12 ounces red seedless grapes
1/4 cup fine sugar

To Serve:
Sugar and whipped cream

Preheat oven to 425F (220C). Grease a deep 10-inch pizza pan or cake pan.

Spread grapes on a baking sheet and bake 10 minutes. Meanwhile, punch down dough and knead with 2 tablespoons sugar. Divide into 2 equal pieces. Roll each piece to a 10-inch circle. Remove grapes from oven; turn off oven.

Place one dough circle in greased pan. Brush surface with water and spoon over half the grapes. Sprinkle with half the remaining sugar. Lay second piece of dough on top and press gently with fingertips to seal dough around grapes and make small pockets.

Spoon remaining grapes over the surface and sprinkle with remaining sugar. Cover with plastic wrap and let rise in a warm place 1-1/2 hours. Preheat oven to 400F (205C). Bake 20 to 25 minutes until golden. Cool, then dust with extra sugar and serve with whipped cream. Makes 6 servings.

Bread Sticks

1 recipe Traditional Pizza Dough, made up to end of step 2, page 8
Sesame or poppy seeds, or cracked wheat, to sprinkle

To Serve:
Slices of prosciutto, if desired

Preheat oven to 400F (200C). Grease several baking sheets.

Punch down dough and knead briefly. Divide dough into approximately 18 equal pieces and roll each piece to an 8-inch length. Arrange on greased baking sheets and brush with water.

Leave plain or sprinkle with sesame or poppy seeds, or cracked wheat, if desired. Bake 15 to 20 minutes until crisp and golden. Cool before serving plain or wrapped with slices of prosciutto, if desired, to serve as a cocktail snack. Makes about 18.

Polenta Bread

1-1/3 cups coarse ground cornmeal
1 cup all-purpose flour
1-1/4 teaspoons salt
1/4 teaspoon pepper
3 tablespoons olive oil
1 cup lukewarm water

To Serve:
Salad

Preheat oven to 425F (220C). Grease a 12-inch pizza pan. In a medium bowl, mix together the cornmeal, flour, salt and pepper. In a small bowl, whisk together 2 tablespoons oil and water. Stir into the flour mixture with a fork to form a grainy paste.

Place in center of pan and press to edges with knuckles. Prick with a fork and brush with remaining oil. Bake 20 minutes until golden. Serve the bread warm with salad. Makes 4 to 6 servings.

Focaccia

1 recipe Traditional Pizza Dough, made up
    to the end of step 2, page 8
1 teaspoon crushed dried rosemary
About 18 pitted green olives
Coarse sea salt, to sprinkle
Rosemary sprigs, to garnish

Preheat oven to 425F (220C). Grease a 12-inch pizza pan.

Punch down dough and knead dough with crushed rosemary. Place dough in center of pan and press to edges with your knuckles. Prick all over with a fork. Press olives into dough. Brush with water and sprinkle with sea salt. Bake 20 minutes until crisp and golden. Garnish with rosemary. Makes 4 to 6 servings.

Variations: Omit green olives and knead chopped ripe olives into dough with rosemary.

Or knead 1/2 cup freshly grated Parmesan cheese into dough and season to taste with a little pepper. In both cases, prick dough with a fork, brush with water and, if desired, sprinkle with sea salt before cooking.

Piadina

2-1/2 cups bread flour
1-1/4 teaspoons salt
1/2 teaspoon baking powder
1/3 cup milk
1/3 cup water
3 tablespoons olive oil

To Serve:
Salami, cheese and salad

In a medium bowl, mix flour, salt and baking powder. In a measuring cup, combine milk and water. Add oil and a little of the water and milk mixture to flour mixture. Stir with a fork and gradually add more liquid until it has all been incorporated. Mix to form a soft dough.

Turn onto a lightly floured surface and knead until smooth. Cover and rest for 15 minutes. Divide dough into 12 equal pieces. Roll each piece out to a 3-inch circle.

Heat a heavy skillet or griddle until a drop of water flicked on the surface bounces and evaporates. Place 2 to 3 circles in skillet and cook 30 seconds. Flip over and continue cooking.

Turn each circle 2 or 3 times until sides are speckled with brown. Place on a wire rack while cooking remaining circles. Serve warm with salami, cheese and salad. Makes 12.

PASTA

TYPES OF PASTA

Certain types of pasta are more suited to a particular dish than others, but pasta of a similar shape may be substituted in any recipe.

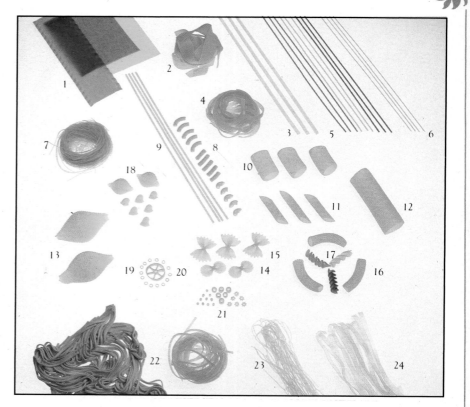

Lasagne (1)
Cooking Time: Some lasagne requires no pre-cooking and is layered straight into a dish with sauce and baked in the oven. Other lasagne must be boiled about 10 minutes before being layered with other ingredients.
Uses: Layered with meat, fish or vegetable sauces. May also be rolled around filling, like cannelloni.

Pappardelle (2)
Cooking time: 8 minutes
Uses: Traditionally served with rabbit sauce.

Tagliatelle (3) & Fettucine (4)
Cooking Time: 6 minutes
Uses: Similar to spaghetti, but particularly good with creamy sauces which adhere better than heavy sauces. May also be fried.

Spaghetti (5)
Cooking time: 12 minutes
Uses: Served simply with butter or oil, or with almost any kind of sauce.

Spaghettini (6)
Cooking time: 8 minutes
Uses: Traditionally served with fish and shellfish sauces. Also good with tomato sauce.

Vermicelli (7)
Cooking time: 5 minutes
Uses: Very thin vermicelli sold in clusters is ideal for serving with very light sauces. Long vermicelli is used in the same way as spaghetti.

Macaroni (8) & Bucatini (9)
Cooking time: 8 to 10 minutes
Uses: Often used in baked dishes, particularly those with a cheese-based sauce.

Rigatoni (10)
Cooking time: 10 minutes
Uses: Generally used in baked dishes. The ridges help the sauce to cling to the pasta. It may also be stuffed.

Penne (11)
Cooking time: 10 minutes
Uses: Served with meat sauces which catch in the hollows.

Cannelloni (12)
Cooking time: Most cannelloni tubes require no pre-cooking and are stuffed directly before baking. If they are to be fried, they should be boiled first 7 to 10 minutes.
Uses: Filled cannelloni may be baked in the oven in a sauce or topped with butter and grated cheese, and may also be deep-fried until crisp.

Conchiglie (13)
Cooking time: Large shells take about 15 minutes to cook and smaller ones about 10 minutes.
Uses: Large shells may be stuffed, and their shape makes a fish filling particularly appropriate. Smaller shells are used in casseroles and soup, and served cold in salads.

Fiochetti (bows) (14) & Farfalle (butterflies) (15)
Cooking time: 10 minutes
Uses: Ideal for serving with meat or vegetable sauces, which become trapped in the folds.

Fusilli (16) & Tortiglioni (spirals) (17)
Cooking time: 10 minutes
Uses: Served with substantial meat sauces, which are trapped in the twists. Also good in salads.

Lumache (18)
Cooking time: 10 minutes
Uses: Similar to conchiglie.

Rotini (wheels) (19) & Anelli (20)
Cooking time: 8 minutes
Uses: Added to savory bakes and salads.

Pastina (anellini, ditalini, stellini) (21)
Cooking time: 8 minutes
Uses: Most often added to soups, but may be used in many other dishes.

Egg Noodles (22)
Cooking time: 4 to 5 minutes
Uses: Flat noodles are often served in soups. Round ones are served in sauces, and are best for stir-frying. Also served as an accompaniment instead of rice.

Rice Noodles (23)
Cooking time: Simply soak in hot water 10 to 15 minutes.
Uses: Served in spicy sauces, soups and stir-fry dishes.

Transparent (Cellophane) Noodles (24)
Cooking time: Soak in hot water 5 minutes.
Uses: Added to soup or deep-fried as a garnish.

Variations

PASTA VERDI:
Cook 4 ounces spinach. Drain, squeeze out as much moisture as possible and chop very fine. Add spinach to the eggs and flour, adding extra flour if necessary.

BASIC PASTA DOUGH
2 eggs
1-1/2 cups bread flour
Pinch salt

Any quantity of pasta may be made by using the proportions of 1 egg to 3/4 cup flour, but the most convenient quantity to handle, particularly for a beginner, is a 2- to 3-egg mixture. Larger amounts should be mixed and rolled in batches.

TOMATO PASTA:
Add 1 tablespoon tomato paste to the eggs and flour.

Beat eggs in a large bowl. Sift flour and salt over eggs. Mix together with a fork, then press into a ball with the hands. It should be firm but pliable, and not sticky. Add more flour if too moist.

HERB PASTA:
Add 1 tablespoon of a single fresh herb, such as parsley, or mixed fresh herbs, to the eggs and flour.

Turn the dough onto a lightly floured surface, and knead firmly 5 to 10 minutes or until smooth. Wrap in a damp towel and let rest 30 minutes at room temperature.

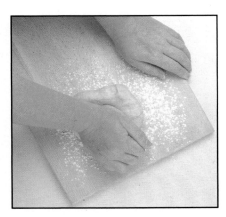

WHOLE-WHEAT PASTA:
Use whole-wheat flour in place of white flour or, for a lighter texture, a mixture of whole-wheat and white flour.

When rolling pasta by hand, you will need a long rolling pin and a large, clear work surface. It is essential to work quickly, or the pasta will dry out and crack. Roll away from you, and keep lifting the sheet of pasta on the rolling pin, turning it 45 degrees as you roll. Lift the far edge on the rolling pin, and push it away from you to stretch the dough.

As the sheet of pasta becomes larger, allow it to hang over the edge of the table to increase the stretch. Eventually, the sheet of pasta should look smooth and suede-like in texture, and it should be so thin that you can read newsprint through it. Unless you are an expert, you will not be able to roll the pasta as thin by hand as with a machine. Therefore you will probably find that you need a slightly larger quantity of pasta than that given in a recipe.

If you are making lasagne or filled pasta, such as ravioli or tortellini, the pasta should be used immediately. Otherwise, it should be spread on a towel and left to dry 30 minutes. Turn it over after 15 minutes. Let dry long enough to prevent it sticking, but not so much that it becomes brittle. The dough is then ready for cutting into shapes.

TAGLIATELLE:
Loosely roll up pasta dough in a cylinder. Using a sharp knife, cut cylinder in even widths. Shake out coils in loose nests. These may be cooked immediately or left to dry for several days before being stored.

LASAGNE & CANNELLONI:
Using a sharp knife or serrated pasta-cutting wheel, cut lasagne sheets to whatever size will best fit your dish. For most purposes, sheets measuring 5" x 4" are the most convenient. For cannelloni, cut pasta as for lasagne. The sheets can then be cooked and rolled around a stuffing before baking in oven.

PAPPARDELLE & FARFALLE:
For pappardelle, using a serrated pasta-cutting wheel, cut pasta in strips 12" long and 3/4" wide. For farfalle, cut pasta sheet in 2" squares with pasta-cutting wheel. Pinch each square together in middle to produce a butterfly effect.

Note: Cut pasta trimmings in pretty shapes with a biscuit or aspic cutter and use for garnishing soups.

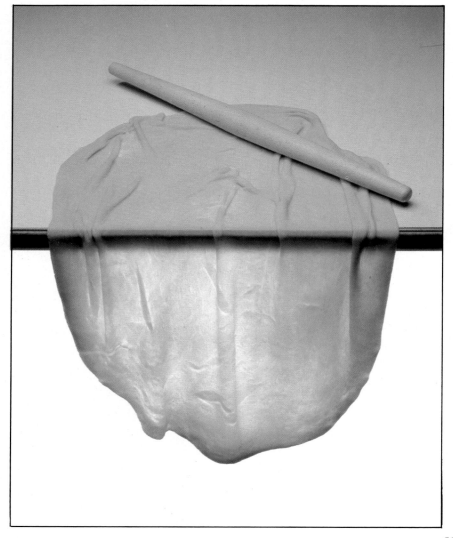

Electric machines are available which mix the dough and then extrude it through the selected cutter, but unless you intend to make large quantitites of pasta on a regular basis, they are not necessary.

The most useful machine is a hand cranking one which rolls the pasta into sheets and has cutters of different widths through which the sheets can be passed. One machine has an attachment for mixing the pasta, but this is not an essential refinement, particularly if you have a food processor. To mix pasta dough in a food processor, process the eggs 30 seconds, then add the sifted flour and salt and process until the mixture forms a ball.

By fitting cutters of various sizes onto your pasta rolling machine, it is possible to cut spaghetti or noodles in several different widths. Do not cut spaghetti into long sheets of pasta which tend to stick together. Place a towel over the back of a chair and spread the spaghetti or noodles out to dry about 30 minutes.

Divide the dough into as many pieces as the number of eggs used. Set the rollers of the machine to the widest setting. Flatten the pieces of dough and roll each through in turn.

Fold each piece in thirds, crosswise, and feed through again. Do this about eight times, or until the sheet of pasta is smooth and silky. Set the rollers one notch closer together and feed the pasta through once on each setting.

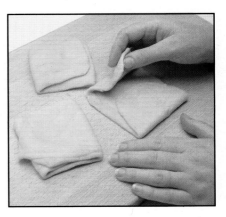

Cut the sheets of pasta in half if they become too long to hand easily. A final rolling on the narrowest but one setting should produce pasta of the correct thickness for most purposes.

MAKING FILLED PASTA

ROUND RAVIOLI:
Cut circles from the filled sheets of pasta using a sharp knife, serrated pasta-cutting wheel or a special round pasta-cutting stamp.

RAVIOLI:
When making ravioli, prepare the filling first and set aside. Then make the dough, see page 51, and roll into strips. Lay the strips out on a towel or floured surface and keep those you are not working on covered with a damp cloth.

HALF MOON RAVIOLI:
Cut circles about 2" in diameter. Place a pea-sized amount of filling in the middle. Fold over 1 side of the circle and press edges firmly together. Leave to dry as for ravioli.

Place small amounts (1/2 teaspoon) of filling at 1-1/2-inch intervals over sheet of pasta and lay a second sheet over the top.

TORTELLINI:
Cut circles about 2 inches in diameter. Place a pea-sized amount of filling slightly to 1 side of the middle. Fold over 1 side of the circle so that it falls just short of the other side and press the edges firmly together. Curve the semi-circle round and pinch the edges together. Let dry in the same way as ravioli.

Press down firmly between the mounds of pasta, and cut between the mounds with a pastry wheel. Spread the ravioli out on a towel to dry about 30 minutes, turning over after 15 minutes. Take care to keep separate, or they will stick together. Round ravioli, or agnolotti, is made by cutting circles from the filled sheets of pasta.

CAPPELLETTI:
Cut 2-inch squares of pasta. Put a small amount of filling in the center of each square. Fold in half diagonally to form a triangle, leaving a slight overlap between the edges. Press firmly to seal. Wrap the long side of the triangle around a finger until the 2 ends overlap. Press the ends firmly together with the points of the triangle upright. Let dry in the same way as ravioli.

Minestrone Soup

3 tablespoons olive oil
4 (1-oz.) thin slices ham, cut into
   matchsticks
1 onion, chopped
2 carrots, chopped
2 celery stalks, chopped
8 oz. white cabbage, coarsely shredded
   (4 cups)
1 medium-size zucchini, diced (2 cups)
4 oz. green beans, cut into 1-inch lengths
6 cups chicken stock
1 (15-oz.) can tomatoes
Salt and pepper
3/4 cup macaroni (4-oz.)
1 tablespoon chopped fresh parsley
Freshly shredded Parmesan cheese

In a large saucepan, heat olive oil. Add ham, onion, carrots and celery. Cook gently until beginning to soften. Add cabbage, zucchini, beans, stock, tomatoes with juice, salt and pepper. Bring to a boil; reduce heat. Cover; simmer about 2 hours. Add macaroni. Cook 10 to 15 minutes or until macaroni is just tender to the bite. Add parsley. Serve with Parmesan cheese. Makes 6 to 8 servings.

Variation:
Vary the vegetables according to taste and availability. Pesto, see page 64, may be stirred in before serving.

White Onion Soup

1/4 cup butter
3 medium-size onions, finely
   sliced (1-1/2 cups)
1 tablespoon all-purpose flour
1-1/4 cups boiling water
3-3/4 cups milk
2 oz. straight vermicelli, broken into
   1/2-inch pieces
Salt and pepper
Fresh parsley, if desired
12 to 18 bacon rolls, if desired

In a medium-size saucepan, melt butter. Add onions. Cook gently until soft. Stir in flour; cook until bubbly. Gradually stir in hot water. Cook, stirring, until sauce is smooth and thickened. Stir in milk. Bring to a boil. Add vermicelli, salt and pepper. Cover pan. Cook, stirring frequently, until vermicelli is just tender to the bite. Place parsley and bacon rolls on wooden picks and garnish soup, if desired. Makes 4 to 6 servings.

Tomato & Pasta Soup

8 medium-size tomatoes
1/4 cup butter
1 medium-size onion, finely chopped
   (1/2 cup)
1/3 cup ditalini or elbow macaroni (2 oz.)
1 quart chicken stock
Pinch of saffron
Pinch of chili powder
Salt
Fresh parsley, if desired

Put tomatoes into a bowl. Cover with boiling water 1 minute. Drain. Cover with cold water 1 minute. Drain. Remove and discard skins and chop tomatoes. In a large saucepan, melt butter. Add onion. Cook until beginning to soften. Add ditalini; cook, stirring, 2 minutes. Add tomatoes. Add stock and saffron. Bring to a boil; reduce heat. Cover; simmer until ditalini is just tender to the bite. Stir in chili powder and salt to taste. Garnish with parsley, if desired. Makes 4 servings.

Light Vegetable Soup

3-3/4 cups vegetable stock, made from
   vegetable trimmings or bouillon
   cube
2 carrots
2 celery stalks, thinly sliced
1-1/2 cups thinly sliced button
   mushrooms (3 oz.)
3/4 cup frozen peas (2 oz.)
2 tablespoons small pasta shells (1 oz.)
Salt and pepper
1 tablespoon chopped fresh parsley

Bring stock to a boil in a medium-size saucepan. With the pointed end of a potato peeler, cut grooves down carrots. Cut into thin slices. Add to stock with celery, mushrooms, peas and pasta. Bring to a boil; reduce heat. Cover pan; simmer about 15 minutes, or until pasta and vegetables are just tender to the bite. Season with salt and pepper and sprinkle .with parsley. Makes 4 servings.

Bean & Pasta Soup

2 tablespoons olive oil
1 medium-size onion, finely chopped
1 garlic clove, crushed
2 carrots, finely chopped
2 celery stalks, finely chopped
1-1/2 quarts chicken stock
Salt and pepper
1-1/2 cups pasta shells (3 oz.)
1 (15-oz.) can pinto beans
Celery leaves, if desired

Heat oil in a medium-size saucepan over medium heat. Add onion, garlic, carrots and celery; cook until soft. Add stock, salt and pepper. Bring to a boil. Cover; simmer 20 minutes. Add pasta; cook 10 minutes more or until pasta is just tender to the bite. Drain beans. Rinse in cold water. Sieve, or process 1/2 of beans in a blender or food processor. Add puréed and whole beans to soup. Stir well. Cook 2 more minutes. Garnish with celery, if desired. Makes 6 to 8 servings.

Avgolemono Soup

1 quart chicken stock
1/3 cup pastina (1-1/2 oz.)
Salt and pepper
2 eggs
Juice of 1 lemon
Lemon slices, if desired
Fresh herbs, if desired

Bring stock to a boil in a small saucepan. Add pastina; season with salt and pepper. Cook 5 minutes or until pastina is just tender to the bite. In a medium-size bowl, beat eggs. Add lemon juice; beat to mix thoroughly. Whisk a ladleful of hot stock into eggs. Pour egg mixture into stock in saucepan. Over a low heat, whisk constantly 3 to 4 minutes or until soup thickens slightly. Garnish with lemon and herbs, if desired. Makes 4 servings.

Note: The soup must not boil or the eggs will scramble.

Smoked Salmon & Avocado Roll

1 bunch watercress
3 green onions, very finely chopped
1 tablespoon olive oil
1 teaspoon prepared horseradish
Salt and pepper
1 avocado
Juice of 1/2 lemon
3 cooked green lasagne noodles
3 oz. smoked salmon, thinly sliced
1/4 cup mayonnaise
1/4 cup crème fraîche
1 tablespoon chopped fresh dill weed
Milk as needed
Lemon peel strips, if desired
Fresh dill, if desired

In a saucepan of boiling water, blanch watercress 10 seconds. Drain; refresh in a bowl of cold water. Squeeze gently in a cloth to dry. Chop fine. In a small bowl, mix together watercress, green onions, olive oil, horseradish, salt and pepper. Halve and pit avocado; peel. Cut in lengthwise slices. Toss avocado in lemon juice. Spread a little watercress mixture over each sheet of lasagne. Lay a slice of smoked salmon on each sheet. Arrange avocado slices in a line down the length of the middle of each sheet. Starting with a long side of pasta, roll up jelly-roll fashion. Wrap each roll in plastic wrap. Chill 2 hours. In a bowl, mix together mayonnaise, crème fraîche, dill weed, salt and pepper. Add a little milk, if necessary, to make a pouring consistency. Cut each roll diagonally in slices 3/4-inch wide. Garnish with lemon peel strips and dill, if desired. Serve with dill sauce. Makes 4 to 6 first course servings.

Seafood Pasta Salad

12 oz. monkfish, skinned
1/4 cup dry white wine
3 oz. smoked salmon trout
4 oz. cooked shrimp, peeled, deveined
4 cups pasta verti spirals (8 oz.), cooked
1/4 teaspoon dried dill weed
Lemon slices, if desired
Fresh dill, if desired

Dressing:
Salt and pepper
1/2 teaspoon dry mustard
1 garlic clove, crushed
1 tablespoon lemon juice
1/3 cup olive oil

Cut monkfish in cubes; put into a small saucepan with wine and enough water to cover. Cook for a few minutes until fish is tender. Drain; let cool. Cut trout in strips. In a large bowl, combine monkfish, trout, shrimp, pasta and dill weed. Make Dressing. Pour Dressing over pasta mixture. Mix thoroughly. Garnish with lemon slices and dill, if desired. Makes 4 servings.

To make Dressing: In a small bowl, mix together salt, pepper, mustard, garlic and lemon juice. Gradually stir in olive oil.

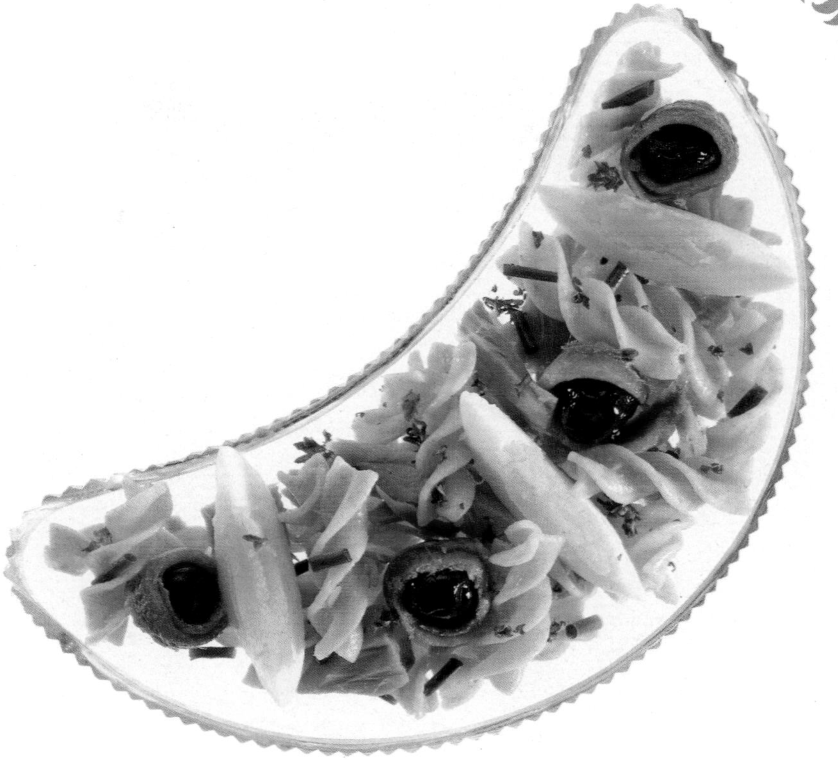

Three-Colored Pasta Salad

6 green onions
1 small red bell pepper, diced
1 small green bell pepper, diced
1 recipe dressing
4 cups red, green and white pasta shells
(8 oz.)

Chop green onions until fine. In a bowl, combine green onions and bell peppers with Dressing. In a large saucepan of boiling salted water, cook pasta until just tender to the bite. Drain; rinse in cold water. Drain thoroughly. In a large bowl, mix together Dressing and pasta. Makes 4 to 6 servings.

Pasta Niçoise

4 cups whole-wheat pasta
spirals (8 oz.)
6 canned anchovies, drained
6 pitted black olives, sliced
1 (6-oz.) can tuna, drained, flaked
1 tablespoon chopped fresh parsley
1 tablespoon chopped chives
1 hard-boiled egg, cut in wedges

Dressing:
Salt and pepper
1 teaspoon Dijon-style mustard
1 garlic clove, crushed
1 tablespoon white wine vinegar
1/3 cup olive oil

In a large saucepan of boiling salted water, cook pasta until just tender to the bite. Drain; rinse in cold water. Drain thoroughly. Cut each anchovy in half lengthwise. Wrap anchovy fillets around olives. Drain tuna. In a large bowl, combine cooked pasta, tuna, parsley and chives. Make Dressing. Pour Dressing over pasta mixture. Mix thoroughly. Arrange olives and egg over pasta mixture. Makes 4 servings.

To make Dressing: In a small bowl, mix together salt, pepper, mustard, garlic, vinegar and oil.

— Tarragon Chicken Salad —

4 cups pasta verdi shells (8 oz.)
1 (3-lb.) broiler-fryer chicken, cooked
8 oz. seedless grapes
1 tablespoon chopped fresh tarragon
1/4 cup mayonnaise
1/4 cup crème fraîche
Salt and pepper
Fresh Italian parsley, if desired

In a large saucepan of boiling salted water, cook pasta until just tender to the bite. Drain; rinse in cold water. Drain thoroughly. Remove meat from chicken; cut in pieces. In a large bowl, mix cooked pasta, chicken pieces, grapes and tarragon. In a small bowl, mix together mayonnaise and crème fraîche. Season with salt and pepper. Pour over chicken; mix thoroughly. Garnish with parsley, if desired, and serve at room temperature. Makes 6 servings.

— Avocado & Orange Pasta Salad —

4 cups pasta bows (8 oz.)
1 large avocado
Grated peel and juice of 1/2 orange
Salt and pepper
Orange slices
Orange peel, if desired
Smoked salmon cornets, if desired
Fresh dill, if desired

In a large saucepan of boiling salted water, cook pasta until just tender to the bite. Drain; rinse in cold water. Drain thoroughly. Halve avocado; remove pit. Scoop out pulp, taking care to scrape all dark green flesh from skin. Put avocado, grated orange peel and juice, salt and pepper into a blender or food processor. Purée until smooth. In a large bowl, combine avocado purée and pasta. Mix until pasta is coated with avocado purée. Top with orange slices. Garnish with orange peel, salmon coronets and dill, if desired. Makes 6 servings as an accompaniment.

Note: Serve soon after making or avocado will discolor.

- Creamy Mushroom & Pea Sauce -

1/3 cup butter
2 cups sliced mushrooms (4 oz.)
2/3 cup crème fraîche
2 egg yolks
1/2 cup grated Parmesan
  cheese (1-1/2 oz.)
Salt, pepper and nutmeg
1/2 (10-oz.) pkg. frozen
  green peas
Hot cooked pasta
Fresh mint, if desired

In a medium-size skillet, melt 2 table-spoons of butter. Add mushrooms. Cook gently until tender. Set aside. In a medium-size bowl, beat together crème fraîche, egg yolks, Parmesan cheese, salt, pepper and nutmeg. In a medium-size saucepan, melt remaining butter. Stir in crème fraîche mixture. Add peas. Cook over very low heat, stirring, until mixture is heated through and begins to thicken slightly. Stir in cooked mushrooms. Serve over pasta at once and garnish with mint, if desired. Makes 4 servings.

— Mascarpone & Walnut Sauce —

1 tablespoon butter
1 cup mascarpone (8 oz.)
Milk as needed
3/4 cup walnuts, coarsely
  chopped (3 oz.)
1/4 cup shredded Parmesan
  cheese (3/4 oz.)

In a small saucepan, melt butter. Gradually stir in mascarpone. Cook over low heat, stirring, until sauce is smooth. If necessary, add a little milk to give a smooth, creamy consistency. Stir in walnuts and Parmesan cheese. Season with salt and pepper and serve at once. Makes 4 servings.

Note: Serve over cooked spaghetti or tagliatelle.

Chicken Liver Sauce

2 tablespoons butter
4 bacon slices, chopped
1 medium-size onion, finely chopped (1/2 cup)
1 garlic clove, crushed
12 oz. chicken livers, chopped (1-1/2 cups)
2 teaspoons all-purpose flour
3/4 cup chicken stock
1 teaspoon tomato paste
Salt and pepper
1 teaspoon chopped fresh marjoram
1/4 cup dairy sour cream
Cooked rigatoni
Fresh marjoram, if desired

In a small saucepan, melt butter. Add bacon, onion and garlic. Cook over medium heat until onion is soft. Stir in chicken livers. Cook, stirring, until livers are no longer pink. Stir in flour. Gradually stir in stock. Add tomato paste, salt, pepper and chopped marjoram. Bring to a boil; reduce heat. Cover pan; simmer 10 minutes. Stir in sour cream and serve with rigatoni. Garnish with marjoram, if desired. Makes about 3 cups sauce.

Rabbit Sauce

1 (about 1-lb.) saddle of rabbit
1 cup dry red wine
1 onion, sliced
1 celery stalk, sliced
1 bay leaf
2 black peppercorns
2 tablespoons vegetable oil
6 bacon slices, chopped
1 onion, finely chopped
1 carrot, finely chopped
2 teaspoons all-purpose flour
2/3 cup Chicken Stock, see page 27
Salt, pepper and nutmeg

Put rabbit in a medium-size bowl; cover with wine. Add sliced onion, celery, bay leaf and peppercorns. Cover bowl. Let marinate, in the refrigerator, 1 to 2 days. In a medium-size saucepan, heat oil. Add bacon, chopped onion and carrot. Cook gently until onion is soft. Remove rabbit from marinade; pat dry. Add to pan; brown all over. Stir in flour. Strain marinade; gradually add to pan with stock. Cover pan; cook over low heat 1-1/2 hours, or until rabbit is very tender. Remove rabbit from pan. Cut meat from bones. Chop into small pieces; return to pan. Makes 4 servings.

Note: This sauce is traditionally served with pappardelle, a wide ribbon pasta.

Shellfish Sauce

1/3 cup olive oil
1 lb. fresh mussels in shells, cleaned
1 garlic clove, crushed
2 shallots, finely chopped
2/3 cup dry white wine
Salt and pepper
1 (8-oz.) can clams, drained
2 tablespoons chopped fresh parsley

In a deep skillet with a cover, heat 3 tablespoons of olive oil. Add mussels. Cover pan; cook over medium heat about 4 minutes until all mussels are open. Discard mussels that do not open. Heat remaining oil in a medium-size saucepan. Add garlic and shallots. Cook until shallots are soft. Drain mussels. Strain cooking liquid; add to shallots with white wine. Bring to a boil. Boil gently, uncovered, until reduced slightly. Season with salt and pepper. Remove most mussels from shells, leaving a few for garnishing. Add mussels and clams to cooking juice. Sprinkle parsley over sauce. Serve at once. Makes 4 servings.

Carbonara Sauce

8 bacon slices
2 tablespoons butter
4 large eggs
1/2 cup grated Parmesan
    cheese (1-1/2 oz.)
2 tablespoons half and half
Salt and pepper
1 tablespoon chopped fresh chives
Cooked spaghetti or tagliatelle

Finely chop bacon. In a medium-size saucepan, melt butter over medium heat. Add bacon. Fry, stirring occasionally, until crisp. In a medium-size bowl, beat together eggs, Parmesan cheese, half and half, salt and pepper. Add to bacon. Cook over medium heat, stirring, until eggs begin to thicken. Stir in chives. Pour sauce over hot spaghetti or tagliatelle. Serve at once. Makes 4 servings.

Salmon & Cream Sauce

2 tablespoons butter
1 pint half and half (2 cups)
1/4 cup grated Parmesan
    cheese (3/4 oz.)
2 cups cooked flaked salmon
1 tablespoon chopped fresh dill
Salt, pepper and nutmeg
Fresh dill, if desired

In a medium-size saucepan, heat butter and half and half over low heat. Bring to just below boiling point. Reduce heat. Simmer gently about 10 minutes or until thickened and slightly reduced. Add Parmesan cheese. Stir in salmon, chopped dill, salt, pepper and nutmeg. Garnish with dill, if desired. Makes 4 servings.

Pesto

1/2 cup fresh basil leaves
1/2 cup pine nuts
2 garlic cloves
Salt
1/2 cup grated Parmesan
    cheese (1-1/2 oz.)
1/2 cup olive oil
Cooked pasta

Put basil leaves, pine nuts, garlic and salt in a blender or food processor. Process until mixture forms a paste. Add Parmesan cheese to basil mixture; process until well blended. Add oil, a little at a time; process until sauce has a creamy consistency. Makes 4 to 6 servings.

Variation
When fresh basil leaves are unavailable, a version of pesto may be made with fresh parsley. Use walnuts instead of pine nuts.

Note: Pesto is used as a sauce for pasta, and is also added to dishes such as minestrone soup to give added flavor.

Lemon & Green Peppercorn Sauce

2 tablespoons butter
2/3 cup half and half
1 to 2 teaspoons green
   peppercorns, drained
Grated peel of 1 lemon
Salt

In a small saucepan, melt butter. Stir in half and half. Lightly crush peppercorns with the back of a spoon. Add to sauce. Stir in lemon peel and salt. Cook over low heat, without boiling, until slightly thickened. Makes 4 servings.

Note: This sauce is ideal for serving with fine capellini.

Tomato Sauce

1 lb. tomatoes (3 to 4 medium-size)
4 teaspoons olive oil
1 onion, finely chopped
1 garlic clove, crushed
1 tablespoon tomato paste
1/2 teaspoon sugar
1 tablespoon chopped fresh basil
Salt and pepper
Fresh basil, if desired

Put tomatoes in a medium-size bowl. Add boiling water to cover. Blanch 1 minute; drain. Peel; chop coarsely. In a medium-size saucepan, heat oil over medium heat. Add onion and garlic. Cook until soft. Stir in chopped tomatoes, tomato paste, sugar, chopped basil, salt and pepper. Cover pan; reduce heat to low and cook about 30 minutes or until thickened. If a thicker sauce is required, heat, uncovered, a few more minutes. Garnish with basil, if desired. Makes 4 servings.

Note: For a smooth sauce, process in a blender or food processor.

—— Spaghetti with Meatballs ——

1 bread slice, crusts removed
Water
1 onion, very finely chopped
1 garlic clove, crushed
1 lb. lean ground beef
1 tablespoon chopped fresh parsley
Salt and pepper
1 tablespoon vegetable oil
1 recipe Tomato Sauce, see page 65
12 oz. spaghetti
1/2 cup grated Parmesan cheese (1-1/2 oz.)
Fresh basil, if desired

Soak bread in a little water. Squeeze dry and crumble into a bowl. Add onion, garlic, ground beef, parsley, salt and pepper. Mix well. Shape in 1-inch balls. Heat oil in a 10-inch skillet over medium heat. Add meatballs. Cook about 10 minutes or until browned all over. Drain off excess fat. Add Tomato Sauce. Cook until heated through. Cook spaghetti, see pages 7-8. Drain well; pour into a heated serving dish. Add meatballs and sauce. Sprinkle with Parmesan cheese. Garnish with basil, if desired, and serve. Makes 4 servings.

—— Ricotta, Leek & Ham Sauce ——

2 tablespoons butter
2 leeks, thinly sliced
1 garlic clove, crushed
4 (1-oz.) thin ham slices
8 oz. ricotta cheese (2 cups)
2/3 cup dairy sour cream
Milk
Pepper
Cooked tagliatelle

In a medium-size saucepan over medium heat, melt butter; add leeks and garlic. Cook until leeks are soft. Cut ham into small squares. Stir into leeks. Cook a few minutes. In a medium-size bowl, mix together ricotta and sour cream. Add a little milk, if necessary, to make a smooth creamy sauce. Season with pepper. Add to pan with leeks and ham. Reduce heat to low; cook until sauce is heated through. Serve at once with tagliatelle. Makes 4 servings.

Béchamel Sauce

1-1/4 cups milk
1/2 bay leaf
1/4 cup butter
1/4 cup all-purpose flour
Salt and pepper

In a small saucepan, heat milk and bay leaf over low heat to just below boiling point. Remove from heat. Remove and discard bay leaf. In a small saucepan, melt butter over medium heat. Stir in flour, cook 2 minutes, stirring constantly. Remove from heat. Gradually stir in hot milk. Return pan to heat. Stir until thick and smooth. Reduce heat to low and cook 10 minutes stirring occasionally. Season with salt and pepper. If sauce is not to be used immediately, cover surface closely with plastic wrap. Makes 4 servings.

Variation
Ham & Mushroom Sauce
6 oz. fresh mushrooms, sliced
   (about 2-1/2 cups)
3 tablespoons dry apple cider
4 oz. ham, cut in shreds (about 1 cup)
Grated nutmeg
Béchamel Sauce made with 1-3/4 cups
   milk, 3 tablespoons each butter and
   all-purpose flour
Hot cooked pasta

In a small saucepan, combine mushrooms with cider. Cover pan. Cook over low heat 5 minutes. Add mushrooms, cooking liquid, ham and nutmeg to Béchamel Sauce. Serve with pasta.

Green & Blue Sauce

8 oz. broccoli
6 oz. Gorgonzola cheese
1/2 cup mascarpone (3-1/2 oz.)
1 cup plain yogurt
Pepper
Hot cooked Pasta Verdi, see pages
   10-11

Wash and trim broccoli, discarding stalks. Cut in small flowerets. Cook in boiling salted water 2 to 3 minutes or until crisp-tender. Drain thoroughly. Roughly chop cheese. Put cheese and mascarpone in a small saucepan. Stir over low heat until cheese has melted. Add broccoli and yogurt to cheese sauce. Heat gently, stirring occasionally, 2 minutes. Pour over pasta. Makes 4 servings.

Mediterranean Sauce

1 medium-size eggplant
Salt
1/4 cup olive oil
1 onion, chopped
1 garlic clove, crushed
1 small green bell pepper
1 small red bell pepper
1 small yellow bell pepper
4 medium-size tomatoes, peeled,
  coarsely chopped
Salt and pepper
1/2 teaspoon dried leaf oregano
Hot cooked spaghetti

Cut eggplant in 3/4-inch strips. Put
into a colander; sprinkle with salt. Let
stand 1 hour. Pat dry with paper towels. In a deep 12-inch skillet with a
cover, heat oil. Add onion and garlic.
Cook over low heat until soft. Add
eggplant. Cook, stirring occasionally,
5 minutes. Cut peppers in 3/4-inch
strips. Add to skillet; cook 5 minutes.
Stir in tomatoes, salt, pepper and oregano. Cover pan and cook gently 20
minutes. Serve with spaghetti. Makes
4 servings.

Bolognese Sauce

2 tablespoons vegetable oil
2 slices bacon, chopped
1 onion, finely chopped
1 carrot, finely chopped
1 celery stalk, finely chopped
1 garlic clove, crushed
8 oz. lean ground beef
4 oz. chicken livers, chopped (1/2 cup)
2 tablespoons tomato paste
1/2 cup dry white wine
1/2 cup beef stock
Salt, pepper and nutmeg
Hot cooked spaghetti
Celery leaves, if desired

In a large saucepan, heat oil over
medium heat. Add bacon; cook until
lightly browned. Add onion, carrot,
chopped celery and garlic to bacon.
Cook, stirring occasionally, until beginning to brown. Add ground beef;
cook, stirring occasionally, until
evenly browned. Stir in chicken
livers; cook until they are no longer
pink. Drain off excess fat. Stir in
tomato paste, wine, stock and season-
ings. Cover and bring to a boil. Cook
over low heat 30 to 40 minutes. Serve
with spaghetti. Garnish with celery
leaves, if desired. Makes about 3
cups.

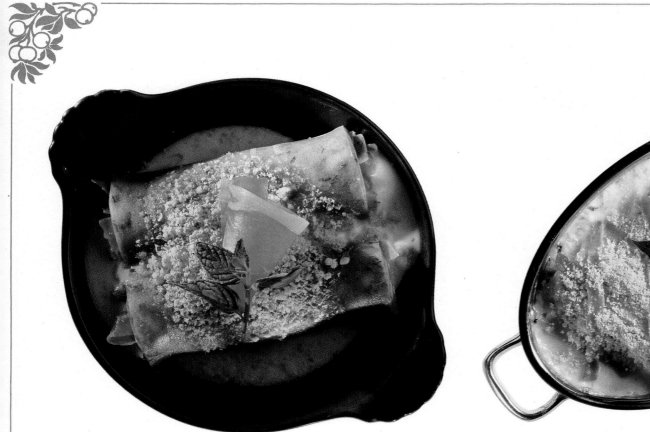

Cannelloni au Gratin

1/4 cup butter
1 medium-size onion, finely chopped
1 garlic clove, crushed
6 cups sliced mushrooms (12 oz.)
1 tablespoon all-purpose flour
3/4 cup crème fraîche
Salt, pepper and nutmeg
Herb Pasta using 1 egg, see page 51
6 very thin prosciutto slices
1/2 cup fresh bread crumbs
1/4 cup grated Parmesan cheese (3/4 oz.)
Additional proscuitto slice, if desired
Fresh mint, if desired

In a medium-size saucepan over low heat, melt butter. Add onion and garlic; cook until soft. Add mushrooms; cook, stirring, until soft and most of liquid has evaporated. Stir in flour; add 1/3 cup of crème fraîche to form a thick sauce. Season with salt, pepper and nutmeg. Preheat oven to 350F (175C). Roll out pasta, see page 52; cut out 6 (5″ x 4″) rectangles. Put a prosciutto slice on each rectangle, spoon some mushroom filling across each 1 and roll up from short end. Pack tightly, seams down, in a greased 1-1/2-quart oblong baking dish. Pour remaining crème fraîche over top and sprinkle with mixed bread crumbs and Parmesan cheese. Bake 20 minutes or until golden and bubbling. Garnish with additional proscuitto slice and mint, if desired. Makes 6 first-course servings.

Spinach & Ham Cannelloni

1 lb. fresh spinach
2 tablespoons butter
1 medium-size onion, finely chopped
1 tablespoon all-purpose flour
2/3 cup milk
4 oz. ham, finely chopped (1/2 cup)
Salt, pepper and nutmeg
8 ready-to-use cannelloni tubes
1 recipe Béchamel Sauce, see page 67
3/4 cup grated Cheddar cheese (3 oz.)
2 (1-oz.) ham slices, cut in strips, if desired
Fresh bay leaves, if desired

In a medium-size covered saucepan, cook spinach in a little water until tender. Drain thoroughly. Chop until fine. In the same saucepan over medium heat, melt butter. Add onion and cook until soft. Stir in flour and cook 1 minute. Gradually stir in milk; boil 1 minute. Stir in spinach, chopped ham, salt, pepper and nutmeg. Using a teaspoon, push spinach mixture into cannelloni tubes. Preheat oven to 425F (220C). In a small saucepan, heat Béchamel Sauce over low heat. Stir in 1/2 cup of the cheese. Pour 1/2 of the sauce into a greased oblong 1-quart baking dish. Arrange cannelloni in a single layer in dish; pour remaining sauce over top. Bake 40 minutes or until golden and bubbling. Arrange ham strips in a lattice pattern on top, if desired, and sprinkle with remaining cheese. Garnish with bay leaves, if desired. Makes 4 servings.

Lobster Shells

Meat from a 1 lb. lobster
2 teaspoons lemon juice
2/3 cup whipping cream
Salt
Red (cayenne) pepper
8 conchiglie (large shells), cooked
1/2 teaspoon grated lemon peel
2 teaspoons chopped fresh dill
Black pepper
Lemon twists, if desired
Fresh dill, if desired

Preheat oven to 375F (190C). Chop lobster meat in coarse pieces. Put into a bowl with lemon juice and 2 tablespoons of whipping cream. Season with salt and red pepper. Mix well together. Fill shells with lobster mixture. Arrange in a greased 1-1/2-quart oblong baking dish. In a bowl, mix together remaining whipping cream, lemon peel and dill. Season with salt and black pepper. Pour over shells. Cover dish with foil. Bake 15 to 20 minutes or until heated through. Baste with sauce halfway through cooking time. Garnish with lemon twists and dill, if desired. Makes 4 first-course servings.

Fish Ravioli in Leek Sauce

8 oz. white fish fillets, such as cod, cooked,
** flaked**
2 canned anchovies, drained, minced
1/4 cup grated Parmesan cheese (3/4 oz.)
Grated peel and juice of 1/2 lemon
1 egg yolk
Pepper and nutmeg
Fresh Pasta, using 3 eggs, see page 51
Chopped fresh parsley, if desired
Blanched shredded leek, if desired
Lemon peel strips, if desired

Leek Sauce:
1 lb. leeks, sliced
1/4 cup butter
2/3 cup fish or chicken stock
2/3 cup dairy sour cream

In a medium-size bowl, mix fish, anchovies, Parmesan cheese, lemon peel and juice and egg yolk. Season with pepper and nutmeg. Process in a blender or food processor until fairly smooth. Roll out pasta dough and, using fish purée as a filling, make ravioli; see page 54. Make sauce. Drop ravioli into boiling water and cook 8 to 10 minutes. Drain and turn into a heated serving dish. Warm sauce and pour over ravioli. Garnish with parsley, leek and lemon peel strips, if desired. Make 6 first-course servings

To make sauce: Melt butter in a medium-size saucepan. Add leeks and stir until coated with butter. Cover pan and cook gently until leeks are soft; add stock. Process mixture in a blender or food processor until smooth. Stir in sour cream.

— Pasta with Spinach & Ricotta — — Ravioli with Butter & Sage —

1 lb. spinach
2 cups ricotta cheese (8 oz.)
1/2 cup grated Parmesan cheese (1-1/2 oz.)
1 egg yolk
Salt, pepper and nutmeg
Fresh Pasta, using 3 eggs, see page 51
1/3 cup butter
**2 tablespoons chopped fresh mixed herbs
   (about 1/2 teaspoon dried mixed herbs)**
2 teaspoons lemon juice

In a large saucepan, cook spinach in a small amount of water until tender. Drain; cool. Squeeze spinach dry; chop in a blender or food processor. Add ricotta cheese, Parmesan cheese, egg yolk, salt, pepper and nutmeg. Process until fairly smooth. Roll out pasta; see page 12. Cut in 2-inch squares. Put 1/2 teaspoon of filling in middle of each square. Fold in half to make a triangle; press edges to seal. Wrap long side of triangle around index finger; press ends together. Leave on a towel to dry, turning after 1 hour. Cook cappelletti in a large saucepan of boiling water 10 to 15 minutes or until tender but firm. In a small saucepan, melt butter; stir in herbs and lemon juice. Drain cappelletti; put into a heated serving dish. Add herb butter sauce; stir thoroughly. Serve at once. Makes 6 first-course servings, 4 main-course servings.

Variation
Use Pasta Verde or Tomato Pasta, see page 51, to make a mixture of different colored pasta. If desired, cut pasta in 2-inch circles instead of squares.

1/3 cup butter
1 medium-size onion, chopped
8 oz. ground pork
8 oz. ground veal
**2 tablespoons tomato paste, dissolved in
   1/4 cup water**
Salt, pepper and nutmeg
1/2 cup fresh bread crumbs
2 egg yolks
1 cup grated Parmesan cheese (3 oz.)
Fresh Pasta, using 3 eggs, see page 51
Fresh sage leaves

To make filling, in a medium-size saucepan, melt 2 tablespoons of butter; add onion and cook until soft. Add meat; cook, stirring until brown. Stir in tomato paste mixture and season with salt, pepper and nutmeg. Cover and simmer 30 minutes. Cool, then process in a blender or food processor until smooth, adding bread crumbs, egg yolks and cheese. Make ravioli; see page 54, filling with meat mixture. Drop ravioli into boiling salted water and cook 15 to 20 minutes or until tender but firm. Drain and place in a heated serving dish. Melt remaining butter, pour over ravioli. Season with pepper and garnish with sage leaves. Serve at once. Makes 6 first-course servings.

Tortellini in Tomato Sauce

2 cups cooked chopped chicken
1/2 cup mortadella (4 oz.)
2 eggs
1/2 cup grated Parmesan cheese (1-1/2 oz.)
Salt, pepper and nutmeg
Fresh Pasta, using 3 eggs, see page 51
1 recipe Tomato Sauce, see page 65
Additional grated Parmesan cheese, if
    desired

In a blender or food processor, chop chicken and mortadella until fine. Add eggs, 1/2 cup Parmesan cheese, salt, pepper and nutmeg; process until fairly smooth. Roll out pasta; see page 52. Using a biscuit cutter, cut out rounds 1-1/2 inches in diameter. Put 1/2 teaspoon of filling in middle of each round. Fold each round in half over filling so that upper edge comes just short of lower edge. Press edges to seal. Curl around index finger, pressing two parts firmly together. Leave on a towel to dry, turning after 1 hour. Cook tortellini in a large saucepan of boiling salted water about 10 minutes or until tender but firm. In a small saucepan, heat Tomato Sauce. Drain tortellini, place in a heated serving dish and pour sauce over top. Sprinkle with additional Parmesan cheese, if desired, and serve. Makes 6 first-course servings, 4 main-course servings.

Vermicelli Flan

2 tablespoons butter
2 small leeks, sliced
6 bacon slices, chopped
4 oz. vermicelli
1/2 cup grated Cheddar cheese (2 oz.)
2/3 cup plain yogurt
2/3 cup half and half
2 eggs, beaten
Salt and pepper
1 medium-size tomato, sliced
Leek leaves, if desired

In a skillet, melt butter. Add leeks and bacon. Cook gently until leeks are tender. Preheat oven to 375F (190C). In a large pan of boiling salted water, cook vermicelli until just tender to the bite. Drain; return to pan. Stir in cheese. Press vermicelli onto bottom and sides of a well-greased 9-inch flan pan. Spread bacon and sliced leeks over pasta base. In a medium-size bowl, beat together yogurt, half and half, eggs, salt and pepper. Pour over bacon and leeks. Arrange tomato slices on top. Bake 30 minutes, or until puffed and golden brown. Remove flan ring and serve warm or cold. Garnish with leek leaves, if desired. Makes 4 servings.

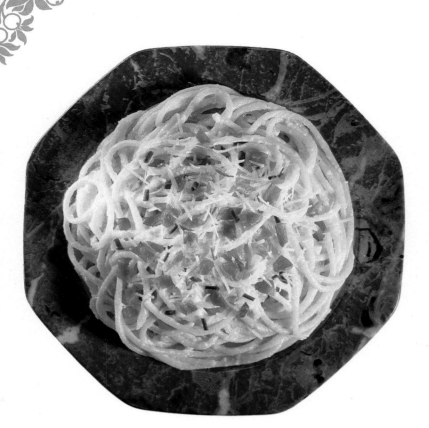

Bucatini with Four Cheeses

6 oz. bucatini
1-1/4 cups half and half
1/2 cup grated Parmesan
   cheese (1-1/2 oz.)
3 oz. Gruyère cheese, cut into small
   dice
3 oz. soft goat's cheese
3 oz. mozzarella cheese, cut into
   small dice
Pepper
Chopped ham, if desired
Chopped chives, if desired

In a large saucepan of boiling salted water, cook bucatini until just tender to the bite. Drain bucatini. Put half and half in a large saucepan with half of Parmesan cheese. Add Gruyère cheese, goat's cheese and mozzarella cheese. Cook over low heat until cheeses are melted. Season with pepper. Add drained bucatini to cheese mixture. Stir well. Sprinkle with remaining Parmesan cheese, ham and chives, if desired. Serve at once. Makes 4 servings.

Lasagne

8 oz. lasagne noodles
1 recipe Béchamel Sauce, see page 67
4 oz. mozzarella cheese, cubed
1 recipe Bolognese Sauce, see page 68
2 tablespoons grated Parmesan cheese
Zucchini slices, if desired
Shredded radicchio, if desired
Endive leaves, if desired

In a large saucepan of boiling salted water, cook noodles, in 2 batches, about 10 minutes or until just tender to the bite. Drain thoroughly. Spread out on paper towels. Preheat oven to 350F (175C). In a saucepan, heat Béchamel Sauce. Add mozzarella cheese; stir until melted. Arrange a noodle layer in bottom of a greased 3-quart oblong baking dish. Spoon half of Bolognese Sauce over top. Cover with noodles. Spread with half of cheese sauce. Repeat layers finishing with remaining cheese sauce. Sprinkle with Parmesan cheese. Bake 30 to 40 minutes or until bubbly. Garnish with zucchini slices, radicchio and endive leaves, if desired, and serve. Makes 4 to 6 servings.

Spinach Pasta Roll

1 tablespoon vegetable oil
1 medium-size onion, finely chopped
2 (10 oz.) pkgs, frozen chopped spinach,
   thawed, drained
2/3 cup cottage cheese
1 cup grated Parmesan cheese (3 oz.)
1 egg yolk
Salt and pepper
1 recipe Fresh Pasta, see page 51
1/4 cup butter
Watercress, if desired

In a 10-inch skillet, heat oil. Add onion; cook until soft. Add spinach; cook 2 minutes, stirring frequently. In a large bowl, mix together cottage cheese, 1/2 of Parmesan cheese, egg yolk, salt and pepper. Stir in spinach and onion. Roll pasta dough in a 14" x 12" rectangle, joining 2 sheets of pasta together if necessary and moistening seam with water. Spread with spinach mixture, leaving a 1/2-inch border around edge. Roll up from long edge. Cut in half to make 2 rolls. Wrap each roll in waxed paper, then foil, leaving seam at top. Turn up ends of foil to form handles. Lay rolls in a deep 10-inch skillet with a cover; add enough water to come halfway up rolls. Bring to a boil; reduce heat. Cover and simmer rolls 30 minutes. Remove from pan; unwrap and cool. Preheat oven to 375F (190C). Cut rolls in 3/4-inch slices. Arrange in a shallow baking dish large enough to hold slices in 1 layer. Melt butter; pour over slices. Sprinkle with remaining Parmesan cheese. Bake 15 minutes or until golden. Garnish with watercress, if desired. Makes 4 servings.

Fish & Pasta Ring

6 oz. tagliatelle verde
2 tablespoons butter
4 eggs, beaten
1-1/4 cups milk
Salt, pepper and nutmeg
1 recipe Tomato Sauce, see page 65
1 lb. white fish fillets, such as cod,
   skinned, cubed
Fresh bay leaves, if desired

In a large saucepan of boiling salted water, cook tagliatelle until just tender to the bite. Drain. Preheat oven to 350F (175C). In a small saucepan, melt butter. Brush a 1-1/2-quart ring mold generously with 1/2 of the melted butter. In a medium-size bowl, beat together eggs, milk, salt, pepper, nutmeg and remaining butter. Pour mixture into buttered ring mold. Spoon drained tagliatelle into ring mold and arrange evenly. Bake in oven 40 minutes or until set. Pour Tomato Sauce into a medium-size saucepan. Bring to a boil; add fish. Simmer gently, uncovered, 5 to 10 minutes or until fish is opaque. Turn out pasta ring onto a large heated serving dish. Spoon some fish sauce into the center; pour a little over top of pasta ring. Arrange remaining fish and sauce around the edge. Garnish with bay leaves, if desired. Makes 4 servings.

Smoked Fish Lasagne

1 lb. smoked fish fillets, such as haddock
2 cups milk
4 medium-size carrots, cut in small dice
4 celery stalks, cut in small dice
1/3 cup butter
2 cups water
6 lasagne verde noodles
1 tablespoon chopped fresh parsley
Salt and pepper
1/2 cup all-purpose flour
Nutmeg
2 tablespoons Parmesan cheese, grated
Lemon slices, if desired
Fresh parsley, if desired

Put fish and milk into a medium-size saucepan. Bring to a boil; reduce heat to low and cook until fish flakes. Combine carrots and celery in a medium-size saucepan with 3 tablespoons of butter and water. Bring to a boil; simmer until vegetables are tender. Meanwhile, in a large saucepan of boiling salted water, cook noodles until just tender to the bite. Drain; spread out on paper towels. Drain fish, reserving cooking liquid. Flake fish into a bowl. Drain vegetables, reserving cooking liquid. Add vegetables to fish with chopped parsley. Season with salt and pepper. Preheat oven to 375F (190C). Make a Béchamel Sauce, see page 67, with reserved fish and vegetable cooking liquids, remaining butter and flour. Season with salt, pepper and nutmeg. Put a layer of noodles in bottom of a greased 2-quart oblong baking dish. Cover with a third of fish mixture, then a third of sauce. Repeat layers twice, ending with sauce. Sprinkle with Parmesan cheese. Bake 25 minutes or until hot and bubbly. Garnish with lemon slices and parsley, if desired, and serve. Makes 4 to 6 servings.

Tuna & Macaroni Layer

1-1/4 cups whole-wheat macaroni (6 oz.), cooked
3/4 cup shredded Cheddar cheese (3 oz.)
1 (7 oz.) can tuna, drained
1/2 recipe Béchamel Sauce, see page 67
2 teaspoons lemon juice
2 hard-cooked eggs, chopped
1 tablespoon chopped fresh parsley
Salt and pepper
Lemon pieces, if desired
Fresh parsley, if desired

Mix macaroni with 1/2 cup of cheese. Set aside. Flake tuna into a small saucepan with Béchamel Sauce, lemon juice, eggs, chopped parsley, salt and pepper. Toss together. Cook over low heat until warmed through. Divide tuna mixture among 4 (10-ounce) flameproof ramekins. Top with macaroni and cheese mixture. Sprinkle remaining 1/4 cup of cheese over top. Broil under medium heat until golden and bubbling. Garnish with lemon pieces and parsley, if desired. Makes 4 servings.

Kidney & Pasta Turbigo

Tomato & Zucchini Pasta Bake

4 lamb kidneys
1/4 cup butter
4 cocktail sausages
4 oz. button mushrooms (2 cups)
24 button onions, peeled
1 teaspoon tomato paste
2 teaspoons all-purpose flour
2/3 cup beef stock
1 tablespoon dry sherry
1 bay leaf
Salt and pepper
3 cups pasta spirals (6 oz.)

Skin and cut kidneys in half; remove core. In a medium-size saucepan, melt butter. Add kidneys and sausages. Cook over medium heat, stirring occasionally, until brown. Remove from pan; set aside. Add mushrooms and onions to saucepan. Cook 5 to 6 minutes, stirring occasionally. Stir in tomato paste and flour. Cook 1 to 2 minutes. Stir in stock and sherry. Bring to a boil. Return kidneys and sausages to saucepan with bay leaf. Add salt and pepper. Cover pan. Reduce heat to low; cook 20 to 25 minutes or until kidneys are tender. Meanwhile, in a large saucepan of boiling salted water, cook pasta until just tender to the bite. Drain. Add to kidney mixture, toss to coat pasta. Makes 4 servings.

3 medium-size zucchini, sliced
4 cups rigatoni (12 oz.)
1 recipe Tomato Sauce, see page 65
8 oz. mozzarella cheese, thinly sliced
1 teaspoon olive oil
Fresh basil, if desired

Bring a small amount of water to a boil in a medium-size saucepan. Add sliced zucchini and cook for a few minutes until crisp-tender. Drain; set aside. Preheat oven to 350F (175C). In a large saucepan of boiling salted water, cook rigatoni until almost tender. Drain; rinse in cold water. Place 1/3 of rigatoni in a buttered 3-quart oblong baking dish. Spread 1/3 of Tomato Sauce, followed by 1/3 of cheese over rigatoni. Repeat layers, then spread zucchini over cheese. Cover with remaining rigatoni, Tomato Sauce and cheese. Sprinkle with olive oil. Bake 20 minutes or until cheese has melted over top. Garnish with basil, if desired. Makes 4 to 6 servings.

Pork & Beans

2 tablespoons vegetable oil
3/4 lb. pork tenderloin, cut in thin slices
1 medium-size onion, chopped
1 garlic clove, crushed
1-1/4 cups whole-wheat pasta grills (6 oz.)
1 (15-oz.) can cannellini beans (white kidney beans), drained
3 tablespoons chopped fresh parsley
3 tablespoons tomato paste
1 quart chicken stock
Salt and pepper
Additional chopped fresh parsley, if desired

In a deep 10-inch skillet with a cover, heat oil. Add pork; cook over medium heat until browned. Remove pork from pan. Set aside. Add onion and garlic to pan; cook until beginning to soften. Return pork to pan, stir in pasta, beans, 3 tablespoons chopped parsley, tomato paste, stock, salt and pepper. Bring to a boil; reduce heat. Cover pan. Simmer, stirring occasionally, about 20 minutes or until pasta is tender and most of liquid is absorbed. Add more stock if liquid is absorbed before pasta is cooked. Sprinkle with additional chopped parsley, if desired, and serve. Makes 6 first-course servings, 4 main-course servings.

Devilled Crab

8 oz. crabmeat
1 teaspoon Dijon-style mustard
2 teaspoons Worcestershire sauce
Juice of 1/2 lemon
Salt and red (cayenne) pepper
1/2 cup plain yogurt
1 cup small pasta shells (2 oz.), cooked
2 tablespoons fresh bread crumbs
1/4 cup grated Parmesan cheese (3/4 oz.)
Lemon peel strip, if desired
Chives, if desired

Preheat broiler. In a medium-size bowl, combine crabmeat, mustard, Worcestershire sauce, lemon juice, yogurt and pasta. Season with salt and red pepper. Divide mixture among 6 scallop shells. In a small bowl, mix together bread crumbs and Parmesan cheese. Sprinkle crumbs over crab mixture. Broil under medium heat about 10 minutes or until golden. Garnish with lemon peel strip and chives, if desired. Makes 6 first-course servings.

Frankfurter Bake

2 tablespoons vegetable oil
1 onion, sliced
2 celery stalks, sliced
6 frankfurters, cut in 1-inch lengths
2 tomatoes, peeled, chopped
2 teaspoons cornstarch
2/3 cup dairy sour cream
1 tablespoon tomato paste
Salt and pepper
3 cups pasta wheels (6 oz.), cooked
Additional sour cream, if desired
Fresh parsley, if desired

In a deep 10-inch skillet, heat oil. Add onion, celery and frankfurters. Cook, stirring occasionally, until onions and celery are soft. Add tomatoes. Cook 5 more minutes. Preheat oven to 425F (220C). In a small bowl, blend cornstarch and a little of the 2/3 cup of sour cream. Stir in remaining 2/3 cup of sour cream. Add to vegetables in skillet with tomato paste, salt and pepper. Stir pasta into vegetable mixture. Pour into a buttered 2-quart oblong dish. Bake 10 minutes or until bubbly. Garnish with additional sour cream and parsley, if desired. Makes 4 servings.

Vermicelli Timbal

4 oz. fine vermicelli
1/2 recipe Béchamel Sauce, see page 67
4 oz. mozzarella cheese
4 oz. ham
1 tablespoon butter
1/4 cup fresh bread crumbs
1 recipe Tomato Sauce, see page 65
Fresh mint, if desired

In a large saucepan of boiling salted water, cook vermicelli until just tender to the bite. Drain. In a medium-size bowl, combine drained vermicelli and Béchamel Sauce. Set aside. Preheat oven to 425F (220C). Butter 6 (6-ounce) custard cups. Coat with 1/2 of bread crumbs. Cut cheese and ham in small dice. Half fill each custard cup with pasta mixture. Divide cheese and ham among cups. Fill cups with pasta mixture. Sprinkle tops with remaining bread crumbs. Bake 15 minutes or until bubbly. Run a sharp knife around inside of cups. Turn out onto warmed serving plates. Serve with Tomato Sauce. Garnish with mint, if desired. Makes 6 servings.

Baked Cod Italienne

2 tablespoons butter
2 cups sliced mushrooms (4 oz.)
1 recipe Tomato Sauce, see page 65
4 (4-to-5-oz.) white fish steaks, such as cod
Salt and pepper
1 cup pasta shells (4 oz.)
8 ripe olives

Preheat oven to 375F (190C). In a medium-size saucepan, melt butter. Add mushrooms; cook gently until soft. Stir in Tomato Sauce. Put fish into a buttered 2-quart oblong baking dish. Season with salt and pepper. Pour tomato and mushroom sauce over fish. Cover dish with foil; bake about 25 minutes or until fish is opaque when tested with a fork. Meanwhile, cook pasta, see page 7, until just tender to the bite. About 5 minutes before fish has finished cooking, arrange pasta around fish, spooning some of sauce over pasta. Garnish with olives and serve. Makes 4 servings.

Broccoli Pasta Soufflé

8 oz. broccoli
3 tablespoons butter
3 tablespoons all-purpose flour
1-1/4 cups milk
3/4 cup shredded Cheddar
  cheese (3 oz.)
Salt, pepper and nutmeg
4 egg whites
3 egg yolks
2 cups pasta shells (4 oz.), cooked

Divide broccoli in small flowerets. Cook in a medium-size saucepan in a small amount of boiling salted water until crisp-tender. Drain. Preheat oven to 400F (205C). In a large saucepan, melt butter; stir in flour. Cook 2 minutes, stirring constantly, over low heat. Gradually stir in milk. Cook, stirring constantly, until sauce thickens. Simmer gently 5 minutes. Stir in cheese. Season with salt, pepper and nutmeg. Let cool slightly. In a large bowl, whisk egg whites until stiff but not dry. Stir egg yolks into cheese sauce, then stir in broccoli and pasta. Stir 1 tablespoon of egg whites into mixture; gently fold in remaining egg whites. Grease a 2-quart soufflé dish (7-3/4" x 3-3/4"). Pour in mixture; bake about 30 minutes or until soufflé is well risen, golden brown and just set in middle. Serve at once. Makes 4 servings.

Note: This mixture may be baked in individual soufflé dishes 20 minutes.

Bolognese Soufflé

3 cups whole-wheat pasta spirals (about
   4-1/2 oz.)
1 recipe Bolognese Sauce, see page 68
3 eggs, separated
1/4 cup grated Parmesan cheese (3/4 oz.)

Preheat oven to 375F (190C). In a
large saucepan of boiling salted
water, cook pasta until just tender to
the bite. Drain well. Stir into Bolognese Sauce. Stir egg yolks into pasta
mixture. In a medium-size bowl, beat
egg whites until stiff. Gently fold into
pasta mixture. Grease a 3-quart soufflé dish. Pour soufflé mixture into
greased dish. Sprinkle with Parmesan cheese. Bake 40 minutes or until
well risen and golden brown. Serve at
once. Makes 4 servings.

Pepper Gratin

2 large red bell peppers
2 large yellow bell peppers
1/2 cup olive oil
1 garlic clove, crushed
4 anchovy fillets, drained, chopped
8 pitted ripe olives, chopped
1 tablespoon capers
Salt and pepper
8 oz. spaghetti
2 tablespoons fresh bread crumbs
2 tablespoons grated Parmesan cheese
Green bell pepper strips, if desired
Additional ripe olives, if desired

Cook bell peppers under broiler.
Turn peppers at intervals until skins
are blistered and blackened. Cool in a
paper bag. Preheat oven to 375F
(190C). Scrape off skins of bell peppers; cut in strips. In a 10-inch skillet,
heat 1/4 cup of olive oil. Add cooked
bell pepper strips and garlic. Cook 2
to 3 minutes or until softened. Stir in
anchovies, chopped olives and capers. Season with salt and pepper. In
a large saucepan of boiling salted
water, cook spaghetti, see pages 7-8.
Drain and return to pan. Toss with 2
tablespoons of remaining olive oil.
Combine bread crumbs and Parmesan cheese; sprinkle half of mixture
over bottom of a 2-quart oblong baking dish. Spoon half of bell-pepper
mixture over bread-crumb mixture.
Cover with cooked spaghetti. Spoon
remaining bell-pepper mixture over
spaghetti, then sprinkle with remaining bread-crumb mixture. Drizzle
with remaining 2 tablespoons of olive
oil. Bake 20 minutes or until golden
brown. Garnish with bell pepper
strips and additional olives, if desired. Makes 4 servings.

Turkey Tetrazzini

1/4 cup butter
4 (1-oz.) thin ham slices, chopped
1 onion, finely chopped
2 cups sliced mushrooms (4 oz.)
1/3 cup all-purpose flour
1-3/4 cups chicken stock
2/3 cup whipping cream
2 tablespoons dry sherry
2 cups cubed cooked turkey
8 oz. red, green and white tagliatelle,
   cooked
Salt, pepper and nutmeg
1/4 cup grated Parmesan cheese (3/4 oz.)
Fresh parsley, if desired

Preheat oven to 350F (175C). In a medium-size saucepan, melt butter over medium heat. Add ham and onion. Cook until onion is soft. Add mushrooms; cook until soft. Stir in flour; cook, stirring constantly, 2 minutes. Gradually stir in stock. Simmer, stirring constantly, until sauce is thickened and smooth. Remove pan from heat. Stir in whipping cream, sherry, turkey and tagliatelle. Season with salt, pepper and nutmeg. Pour into a greased 2-quart baking dish. Sprinkle with Parmesan cheese. Bake 30 minutes or until golden brown. Garnish with parsley, if desired. Makes 4 servings.

Fish & Pasta Pie

12 oz. smoked haddock
12 oz. fresh haddock
1-3/4 cups milk
1-1/4 cups water
2 tablespoons butter
2 tablespoons all-purpose flour
1 teaspoon lemon juice
3 hard-cooked eggs, sliced
Salt and pepper
1 tablespoon chopped fresh parsley
1 cup plain yogurt (8 oz.)
2 eggs, beaten
1-3/4 cups macaroni (6 oz.), cooked
1 cup shredded Cheddar
   Cheese (4 oz.)
Lemon slices, if desired, cut in half
Fresh parsley, if desired

Put smoked and fresh haddock in a medium-size saucepan with milk and water. Poach 5 to 10 minutes until fresh haddock is opaque when tested with a fork. Reserve 1-1/4 cups of cooking liquid. Preheat oven to 375F (190C). Melt butter in a medium-size saucepan. Stir in flour; cook, stirring constantly, 2 minutes. Stir in reserved cooking liquid. Cook until thickened, stirring constantly. Add fish, lemon juice, hard-cooked eggs and chopped parsley. Season with salt and pepper. Pour mixture into a 2-quart casserole. In a medium-size bowl, mix together yogurt and beaten eggs. Stir in macaroni and 1/3 cup of cheese. Pour over fish mixture. Sprinkle with remaining cheese. Bake 25 to 30 minutes or until golden brown. Garnish with lemon slices and parsley, if desired. Makes 4 to 6 servings.

Stuffed Peppers

1 cup pasta spirals (2 oz.), cooked
1/2 recipe Tomato Sauce, see page 65
2 teaspoons capers
6 pitted ripe olives, chopped
2 red bell peppers
2 yellow bell peppers
2 teaspoons olive oil
Fresh basil leaves, if desired

Preheat oven to 375F (190C). In a medium-size bowl, mix together pasta, Tomato Sauce, capers and olives. Slice off the stem end of peppers. Remove core and seeds. Fill peppers with pasta and tomato mixture. Replace tops of peppers. Put peppers in a buttered 1-1/2-quart oblong baking dish. Pour a little olive oil over each. Bake about 30 minutes or until peppers are tender. Garnish with basil leaves, if desired, and serve. Makes 4 servings.

Beef & Macaroni Strudel

1 cup macaroni (4 oz.)
2 tablespoons vegetable oil
1 onion, finely chopped
8 oz. lean ground beef
1 tablespoon tomato paste
1/2 teaspoon ground cinnamon
1 tablespoon chopped fresh parsley
Salt and pepper
1/2 recipe Béchamel Sauce, see page 48
1/4 cup butter
4 sheets filo pastry
Tomato wedges, if desired
Onion slices, if desired, separated in rings
Fresh parsley, if desired

In a large saucepan of boiling salted water, cook macaroni until just tender to the bite. Drain macaroni. Preheat oven to 375F (190C). In a 10-inch skillet, heat oil. Add onion; cook until soft. Add beef; stir until evenly browned. Drain off excess fat. Stir in tomato paste, cinnamon, chopped parsley, salt and pepper. Stir cooked macaroni into beef mixture with Béchamel Sauce. In a small saucepan, melt butter. Brush a sheet of filo pastry with butter. Lay another sheet of pastry on top. Brush with more butter. Repeat with remaining pastry. Place macaroni mixture in a line along 1 long edge of pastry, leaving a space at each end. Tuck ends over, roll up firmly. Place on a large baking sheet. Brush rolls with butter. Bake 45 minutes or until brown and crisp, brushing with butter occasionally. Garnish with tomato wedges, onion rings and parsley, if desired, and serve. Makes 4 servings.

Variation
Make individual strudels, if desired, and bake for 20 to 25 minutes.

— Spicy Vegetables & Noodles —

2 tablespoons vegetable oil
1 garlic clove, crushed
1 (1/2-inch) cube ginger root, grated
1/2 lb. spinach, coarsely chopped
8 oz. white cabbage, shredded
1-1/4 cups chicken stock
1 tablespoon soy sauce
1 teaspoon chilli sauce
4 oz. fine egg noodles

In a wok or deep 10-inch skillet, heat oil. Add garlic and ginger. Cook, stirring constantly, 1 minute. Add spinach and cabbage. Cook, stirring constantly, until vegetables are bright green and almost tender. Stir in stock, soy sauce and chili sauce. Stir in noodles. Simmer a few minutes until noodles are tender. Makes 4 servings.

Note: Serve as an accompaniment to a meat or chicken dish.

— Spicy Sesame Noodles —

2 tablespoons sesame seeds
1 tablespoon sesame oil
4 teaspoons peanut butter
2 tablespoon soy sauce
2 teaspoons chili sauce
1/2 teaspoon sugar
1/4 cup water
8 oz. rice vermicelli
Carrot blossoms, if desired
Toasted sesame seeds, if desired

In a 6-inch skillet, brown sesame seeds over medium heat. Crush slightly. In a bowl or food processor, mix together browned sesame seeds, sesame oil, peanut butter, soy sauce, chili sauce, sugar and water. Set aside. Put vermicelli into a medium-size bowl. Cover with boiling water. Soak 10 minutes. Drain thoroughly. Put drained vermicelli and sesame sauce in a 2-1/2-quart saucepan. Mix together to coat vermicelli in sauce. Cook over low heat until thoroughly heated through. Garnish with carrot blossoms and sesame seeds, if desired. Makes 4 servings.

Singapore Noodles

2 tablespoons vegetable oil
2 cups sliced mushrooms (4 oz.)
1 onion, finely chopped
1 garlic clove, crushed
4 oz. ham, cut in shreds (1/2 cup)
1 (1-inch) cube ginger root, grated
8 oz. rice vermicelli
1 teaspoon curry powder
Salt
2 cups shredded cooked chicken
4 oz. cooked peeled deveined shrimp
   (3/4 cup)
1/4 cup frozen green peas, thawed
1/3 cup chicken stock
4 teaspoons soy sauce
1/4 cup dry sherry
Green onion daisies, if desired

In a deep 10-inch skillet, heat vegetable oil. Add mushrooms, onion, garlic, ham and ginger. Stir well. Cook over low heat 15 minutes. Put vermicelli into a bowl. Cover with boiling water. Soak 10 minutes. Drain thoroughly. Stir curry powder and salt into mushroom-ham mixture. Add chicken, shrimp, green peas, stock, soy sauce and sherry; stir thoroughly. Add noodles; stir over low heat until heated through. Garnish with green onion daisies, if desired. Makes 4 servings.

Buckwheat Noodles with Eggs

12 oz. buckwheat noodles
2 tablespoons vegetable oil
1 onion, chopped
4 cups shredded Chinese
   cabbage (6 oz.)
4 eggs, beaten
Salt and pepper
1 tablespoon soy sauce
Fresh bay leaf, if desired
Lemon peel rose, if desired

In a large saucepan of boiling salted water, cook noodles in the same way as spaghetti until tender. Drain. Meanwhile, in a large saucepan, heat oil. Add onion; cook until soft. Add Chinese cabbage; cook until beginning to soften. Stir in eggs. Cook, stirring, about 1 minute or until eggs are beginning to set. Stir drained noodles into egg mixture. Add salt, pepper and soy sauce. Garnish with bay leaf and lemon peel rose, if desired, and serve at once. Makes 4 servings.

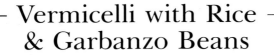

Vermicelli with Rice & Garbanzo Beans

2/3 cup dried garbanzo beans (chick
   peas), soaked overnight in water
   to cover
1/4 cup butter
1 onion, finely chopped
6 oz. vermicelli
1-1/4 cups long-grain rice
2-1/2 cups water
Salt
1/3 cup sour cream
Fresh Italian parsley, if desired

Drain beans; rinse in cold water. Put
into a medium-size saucepan with
cold water to cover. Bring to a boil;
reduce heat. Cover pan. Cook over
low heat 30 minutes or until beans
are tender. Meanwhile, in a large
saucepan, melt butter. Add onion;
cook gently until tender. Break vermicelli into 1-inch pieces. Add to pan.
Stir until well-coated with butter.
Add rice; cook, stirring, until grains
are transparent. Add water and salt
to taste. Bring to a boil. Cover pan
tightly. Reduce heat to low; simmer
about 25 minutes or until water is
absorbed and rice is tender. Add
more water if needed. Stir beans into
vermicelli and rice. Cook over low
heat until heated through. Spoon
sour cream on top. Garnish with
parsley, if desired. Makes 6 servings.

Baked Spaghetti & Eggplant

2 medium-size eggplants, sliced
Salt
Olive oil
1 lb. spaghetti, cooked
1 recipe Tomato Sauce, see page 65
3 hard-cooked eggs, thinly sliced
3/4 cup grated Parmesan cheese (2-1/4 oz.)
Chopped hard-cooked egg, if desired

Arrange sliced eggplants in a colander. Sprinkle with salt; drain at
least 30 minutes. Preheat oven to
375F (190C). Remove eggplant slices
from colander and pat dry. In a large
skillet, heat 2 tablespoons olive oil.
Fry eggplant in batches until very
tender, adding more oil as necessary.
Drain on paper towels. In a large
bowl, mix together spaghetti and
Tomato Sauce. Spread a third of
spaghetti mixture in a greased 4-
quart oblong baking dish. Cover with
half of eggplant slices and half of egg
slices. Sprinkle with a third of Parmesan cheese. Repeat layers, finishing
with a layer of spaghetti. Sprinkle
with remaining Parmesan cheese.
Bake 30 minutes or until golden.
Garnish with chopped egg, if desired.
Makes 6 servings.

— Vegetable Casserole —

2 tablespoons vegetable oil
1 onion, thinly sliced
2 teaspoons all-purpose flour
1 tablespoon paprika
1 (15-oz.) can tomatoes
Water
3 cups cauliflowerets
2 carrots, coarsely chopped
1/2 green bell pepper, coarsely
   chopped
2 medium zucchini, cut in thick
   diagonal slices
2 cups whole-wheat pasta shells (4 oz.)
Salt and pepper
2/3 cup plain yogurt
Fresh Italian parsley, if desired

In a saucepan, heat oil. Add onion;
cook until soft. Stir in flour and paprika. Cook, stirring, 1 minute. Add
tomatoes with juice and water. Bring
to a boil. Stir in cauliflowerets, carrots, bell pepper, zucchini and pasta.
Season with salt and pepper. Cover
pan; simmer 40 minutes or until pasta is tender. Gently stir yogurt into
vegetable mixture. Garnish with
parsley, if desired. Makes 4 servings.

— Macaroni & Vegetable Bake —

1 cup thinly sliced leeks
2 celery stalks
1 red bell pepper
3/4 cup whole-wheat macaroni (4 oz.),
   cooked
2/3 cup plain yogurt
1 cup low-fat soft cheese (4 oz.)
Salt and pepper
2 teaspoons soy sauce
1/2 cup shredded Cheddar
   cheese (2 oz.)

Preheat oven to 350F (175C). Put
leeks into a saucepan of boiling water.
Bring back to a boil. Drain. Finely
chop celery and bell pepper. In a
medium-size bowl, mix together
leeks, celery, bell pepper and macaroni. In another bowl, mix together
yogurt, soft cheese, salt, pepper and
soy sauce. Pour over macaroni mixture. Mix together thoroughly. Put
into an ovenproof dish; cover with
Cheddar cheese. Bake 30 minutes or
until golden and bubbling. Makes 4
servings.

— Vegetarian Bolognese Sauce —

2-3/4 cups water
1 cup lentils (6 oz.)
2/3 cup split peas (4 oz.)
2 tablespoons vegetable oil
1 onion, finely chopped
1 garlic clove, crushed
1 carrot, finely chopped
1 celery stalk, finely chopped
1 (15-oz.) can tomatoes, drained,
    chopped
1 teaspoon dried leaf oregano
Salt and pepper

In a medium-size saucepan, bring water to a boil. Stir in lentils and split peas. Simmer, covered, about 40 minutes or until all liquid has been absorbed and lentils and peas are soft. In a medium-size saucepan, heat oil. Add onion, garlic, carrot and celery. Cook over low heat, stirring occasionally, until soft. Stir in tomatoes and oregano. Season with salt and pepper. Cover pan; simmer gently 5 minutes. Add cooked lentils and split peas to vegetable mixture. Cook, stirring occasionally, until well combined and heated through. Makes 4 to 6 servings.

Note: Serve with whole-wheat spaghetti, if desired.

— Pasta & Vegetable Loaf —

2-1/2 cups water
2/3 cup lentils (4 oz.)
2/3 cup split peas (4 oz.)
1/4 cup butter
1 onion, chopped
1 garlic clove, crushed
1 large carrot, chopped
1 celery stalk, chopped
2 cups small whole-wheat pasta
    shapes (4 oz.), cooked
1 egg, beaten
1/2 teaspoon ground cumin
2 tablespoons chopped fresh parsley
Salt and pepper

In a medium-size saucepan, bring water to a boil. Stir in lentils and split peas. Simmer, covered, about 40 minutes or until all liquid has been absorbed and lentils and peas are soft. Preheat oven to 375F (190C). In a saucepan, heat butter. Add onion, garlic, carrot and celery. Cook, stirring occasionally, until soft. Add cooked lentils and split peas, pasta, egg, cumin and parsley. Season with salt and pepper. Mix together thoroughly. Spoon mixture into a greased 9" x 5" loaf pan. Cover top with foil. Bake 40 minutes. Let stand in pan 5 minutes. Run a knife around edge of loaf and turn out onto a serving dish. Makes 4 servings.

Note: This loaf may be served hot with tomato sauce or cold with salad.

Vegetarian Lasagne

1 cup adzuki beans (6 oz.), soaked
   overnight
4 cups cold water
6 to 8 whole-wheat lasagne noodles
2 tablespoons vegetable oil
1 onion, finely chopped
1 garlic clove, crushed
8 oz. white cabbage, coarsely shredded
   (4 cups)
2 cups sliced mushrooms (4 oz)
1 leek, coarsely chopped
1/2 green bell pepper, coarsely chopped
1 (15-oz.) can tomatoes
1 teaspoon dried leaf oregano
Salt and pepper
1 recipe Béchamel Sauce, see page 67, made
   with whole-wheat flour
1/2 cup shredded Cheddar cheese (2 oz.)
Fresh tarragon, if desired

Drain adzuki beans. Put into a saucepan with cold water. Bring to a boil.

Cover pan; reduce heat. Simmer 40
minutes or until tender. Cook noodles, see pages 7-8. Drain; lay on
paper towels. In a large saucepan,
heat oil. Add onion and garlic. Cook
until soft. Stir in cabbage, mushrooms, leek and bell pepper. Cook 5
minutes, stirring occasionally. Drain
adzuki beans, reserving cooking liquid. Add beans to vegetables. Stir in
tomatoes with juice and 1 cup of
cooking liquid from beans. Add oregano. Season with salt and pepper.
Cover pan; simmer gently 30 minutes, stirring occasionally. Preheat
oven to 350F (175C). In a greased
baking dish, layer noodles, vegetables
and Béchamel sauce, ending with a
layer of sauce. Sprinkle cheese over
top. Bake 30 minutes or until golden
and bubbling. Garnish with tarragon,
if desired. Makes 4 to 6 servings.

Note: Serve with a carrot salad.

Pasta Pan Fry

2 tablespoons vegetable oil
1 onion, chopped
1 green bell pepper, chopped
2 cups sliced mushrooms (4 oz.)
8 oz. chicken livers, chopped (1 cup)
8 oz. tomatoes, peeled, chopped
Salt and pepper
2 fresh sage leaves, chopped
4 cups pasta bows (8 oz.), cooked
Additional fresh sage leaves, if desired

In a large skillet, heat oil. Add onion
and bell pepper; cook, stirring occasionally, 5 minutes or until soft. Add
mushrooms. Cook, stirring, 2 minutes. Add chicken livers. Cook, stirring, until livers are no longer pink.
Stir in tomatoes, salt, pepper and
chopped sage leaves. Cook, stirring,
until the juice begins to run from
tomatoes. Add pasta bows; cook for a
few minutes until heated through.
Garnish with additional sage leaves, if
desired. Makes 4 servings.

Golden Macaroni Fritters

1/2 cup macaroni (2 oz.)
2 eggs
1 cup shredded Cheddar cheese (4 oz.)
2/3 cup canned whole-kernel corn, drained
Salt and pepper
Vegetable oil for deep-frying
Italian parsley, if desired

Cook macaroni in boiling salted water until just tender to the bite. Drain and rinse with cold water. In a medium-size bowl, beat eggs; add cooked macaroni, cheese and corn. Season with salt and pepper. Stir thoroughly. In a deep skillet, heat oil to 375F (190C). Drop tablespoonfuls of macaroni mixture into hot oil. Fry until each fritter is crisp and golden on underside and upper side is set. Turn and fry until other side is crisp and golden. Drain on paper towels. Garnish with parsley, if desired, and serve. Makes 4 servings.

Deep-Fried Ravioli

1 (10-oz.) pkg, frozen chopped spinach, cooked, drained
1-1/3 cups chopped cooked chicken
2 egg yolks
1/3 cup grated Parmesan cheese (1 oz.)
Salt, pepper and nutmeg
Fresh Pasta, using 3 eggs, see page 51
Vegetable oil for deep-frying
Lemon and lime slices, if desired
Fresh parsley, if desired

Squeeze as much water as possible from spinach. In a blender or food processor, process spinach, chicken, egg yolks and Parmesan cheese until quite smooth. Season with salt, pepper and nutmeg. Roll out pasta dough, see page 54. Using chicken mixture as a filling, make ravioli, see page 16. In a deep fryer, heat oil to 375F (190C) or until a 1-inch bread cube turns golden in 40 seconds. Fry ravioli in batches until crisp and golden brown, Drain on paper towels. Garnish with lemon and lime slices and parsley, if desired, and serve. Makes 4 servings

Pizza-Style Spaghettini

8 oz. spaghettini
1 cup shredded Cheddar cheese (4 oz.)
2 eggs, beaten
4 oz. salami, diced (2/3 cup)
1/2 teaspoon dried leaf oregano
Salt and pepper
2 tablespoons vegetable oil
2 tomatoes, sliced
6 ripe olives
Fresh oregano, if desired

Cook spaghettini, see pages 7-8. Drain; rinse with cold water. In a large bowl, using hands, mix together spaghettini, cheese, eggs, salami and dried oregano. Season with salt and pepper. In a medium-size skillet, heat oil. Spoon spaghettini mixture into pan; pat out evenly. Cook about 5 minutes or until underside is brown and crisp and top is set. Turn over onto a plate; slide back into pan. Cook second side until brown and crisp. Turn out onto a large serving plate. Garnish with tomato slices, olives and fresh oregano, if desired. Makes 4 to 6 servings.

Crispy Cannelloni

8 cannelloni tubes
2 tablespoons vegetable oil
1 leek, finely chopped
8 oz. low-fat soft cheese
4 oz. mortadella, chopped
1 teaspoon tomato paste
2 eggs
1 tablespoon chopped fresh parsley
Salt and pepper
1/3 cup fresh bread crumbs
1/3 cup grated Parmesan cheese (1 oz.)
Vegetable oil for deep-frying
Lemon slices, if desired, cut in half
Fresh parsley, if desired

In a large pan of boiling salted water, cook cannelloni 4 to 5 minutes or until almost soft. Drain, rinse with cold water and spread out on paper towels. In a small skillet, heat oil. Add leek; sauté until soft. In a medium-size bowl, mix together leek, soft cheese, mortadella, tomato paste, 1 of the eggs, parsley, salt and pepper. Using a teaspoon, push filling into cannelloni. Mix together bread crumbs and Parmesan cheese. Spread out on a large plate. Beat remaining egg in a flat bowl. Roll cannelloni in beaten egg and coat with bread crumb mixture. In a deep fryer, heat oil to 375F (190C) or until a 1-inch bread cube turns golden in 40 seconds. Fry cannelloni, 4 at a time, 2 to 3 minutes or until crisp and golden. Drain on paper towels. Keep hot while frying remaining cannelloni. Garnish with lemon slices and parsley, if desired. Makes 4 servings.

Crispy Noodles & Onions

**1-2/3 cups short cut noodles
  (6 oz.), cooked
Vegetable oil for deep-frying
1 large Spanish onion,
  thinly sliced
1/3 cup milk
2 tablespoons all-purpose flour
Salt
Green onion daisy, if desired
Lemon butterfly, if desired**

In a deep fryer, heat oil to 375F
(190C) or until a 1-inch bread cube
turns golden in 40 seconds. Fry noodles in 4 batches until crisp and gold-
en. Drain on paper towels. Keep hot.
Separate onion slices in rings. Dip onion rings into milk; toss in flour. Fry
onion rings in 2 batches until crisp
and golden. Mix with noodles;
sprinkle with salt. Garnish with green
onion daisy and lemon butterfly, if
desired, and serve at once. Makes 4
servings as an accompaniment.

Variation
Substitute green noodles for part of
plain noodles.

Noodle Pancakes

**1 oz. noodles, cooked
2 (1-oz.) thin ham slices
2 eggs, beaten
1 tablespoon chopped fresh parsley
1 tablespoon grated Parmesan cheese,
Salt and pepper
Vegetable oil for deep-frying
Lemon slices, if desired
Fresh parsley, if desired**

Chop noodles and ham. In a
medium-size bowl, mix chopped
noodles and ham with eggs, parsley
and Parmesan cheese. Season with
salt and pepper. In a deep skillet,
heat oil. Drop tablespoonfuls of noodle mixture into hot oil. Cook until
underside is crisp and brown; turn
over and fry other side. Remove and
drain on paper towels. Garnish with
lemon slices and parsley, if desired,
and serve at once. Makes 4 servings.

—— Chocolate & Nut Bows ——

3-1/2 cups pasta bows (8 oz.)
1/4 cup blanched almonds
1/4 cup hazelnuts
2 tablespoons butter
2 squares semisweet chocolate,
  coarsely chopped
2 tablespoons light-brown sugar

In a large pan of boiling salted water, cook pasta bows until just tender to the bite. Meanwhile, put nuts in a broiler pan; broil, stirring frequently, until golden brown. Chop nuts coarsely. Drain pasta; put into a warmed serving dish. Stir in butter. Add chopped nuts, chocolate and brown sugar. Toss to mix thoroughly. Serve at once. Makes 4 servings.

Note: Substitute Farfalle (pasta butterflies) for pasta bows, if desired.

Almond Ravioli & Raspberry Sauce

1-1/4 cups ground almonds
1/2 cup powdered sugar
2 egg yolks
2 tablespoons butter
1 recipe Fresh Pasta, see page 51
Plain yogurt
Raspberry leaves, if desired

Raspberry Sauce:
4 cups raspberries
1/2 cup powdered sugar

In a bowl, mix together ground almonds, powdered sugar and egg yolks. In a small saucepan, melt butter. Add to almond mixture. Roll out pasta dough, see page 52. Make ravioli, see page 54, filling with ground almond paste. In a large pan of boiling water, cook ravioli about 10 minutes or until tender but firm; drain. Make sauce. Pour a pool of sauce on 4 dessert plates and arrange ravioli on top. Spoon yogurt into a pastry bag fitted with a plain tip. Pipe a circle of yogurt around each dish. Using a skewer, make a web effect. Decorate with reserved raspberries and raspberry leaves, if desired. Makes 4 servings.

To make sauce: Reserve a few raspberries for decoration. Mix remaining raspberries and sugar in a medium-size saucepan. Heat gently until juice begins to run. Press through a sieve.

Apple Lasagne

1-1/4 cups milk
1 egg
1 egg yolk
1 tablespoon cornstarch
1 tablespoon powdered sugar
1-3/4 lbs. cooking apples
2 tablespoons butter
1/3 cup powdered sugar
Water
1/4 cup raisins
1/2 teaspoon apple pie spice
6 lasagne noodles
1/4 cup walnuts, finely chopped
Powdered sugar, if desired
Whipped cream, if desired

In a medium-size saucepan, heat milk. In a medium-size bowl, mix together egg, egg yolk, cornstarch and 1 tablespoon powdered sugar. Pour hot milk into egg mixture while stirring. Return to saucepan; cook over medium low heat, stirring constantly, until thickened. Set aside. Peel, core and slice apples. Put into a medium-size saucepan with butter, 1/3 cup powdered sugar and a little water. Cook 10 minutes or until apples are soft. Stir in raisins and apple pie spice. Preheat oven to 375F (190C). In a large pan of boiling water, cook noodles, see pages 7-8; drain. In a buttered baking dish, layer lasagne and apple mixture, ending with an apple layer. Pour custard over apples. Sprinkle with walnuts. Bake 25 minutes or until set. Decorate with powdered sugar and serve with a dollop of whipped cream, if desired. Makes 4 servings.

Apricot & Walnut Layer

1 cup dried apricots, soaked overnight
  in water to cover (or cover with
  boiling water; let stand 3 minutes)
1 (1-inch) piece cinnamon stick
Juice and grated peel of 1 orange
1/2 cup packed brown sugar
2 teaspoons cornstarch
Water
1/4 cup butter
1/2 cup fine fresh bread crumbs
4 oz. tagliatelle, cooked
1/2 cup ground walnuts
Walnut halves, if desired
Additional apricot pieces, if desired
Orange-flavored sour cream, if desired

Drain apricots, reserving liquid. Put apricots, 2 tablespoons of apricot liquid, cinnamon, orange juice and peel and 2 tablespoons of brown sugar into a medium-size saucepan. Bring to a boil; reduce heat. Simmer, covered, 10 to 15 minutes or until apricots are tender. Blend cornstarch with a little water. Add to apricots. Cook gently, stirring constantly, until mixture has thickened. Cool. Preheat oven to 375F (190C). Butter a soufflé dish with 2 tablespoons of butter; coat with bread crumbs. Put a third of pasta into dish. Cover with apricot mixture. Cover with half of remaining pasta. Mix together ground walnuts and remaining brown sugar; spread over pasta. Top with remaining pasta. In a saucepan, melt remaining 2 tablespoons of butter. Pour over pasta. Bake in oven 25 minutes. Turn out onto a serving dish. Garnish with walnut halves and additional apricot pieces, if desired. Serve with sour cream, if desired. Makes 4 to 6 servings.

Date & Noodle Pudding

2/3 cup plain yogurt
1/2 cup mascarpone (4 oz.)
1 teaspoon cornstarch
3 eggs, beaten
2 tablespoons honey
1 teaspoon ground cinnamon
1/3 cup chopped dates
1/3 cup golden raisins
1/3 cup candied cherries, chopped
8 oz. tagliatelle, cooked
Whipped cream, if desired
Glacé cherries, if desired

Preheat oven to 350F (175C). In a medium-size bowl, mix together yogurt, mascarpone, cornstarch, eggs, honey, cinnamon, dates, raisins and candied cherries. Add tagliatelle to fruit mixture. Stir well to distribute fruit evenly. Spoon into a greased round baking dish. Level the surface. Bake about 40 minutes or until set and golden brown. Serve warm or cold, decorated with whipped cream and glacé cherries, if desired. Makes 4 servings.

Pear & Pasta Pudding

2/3 cup macaroni (3 oz.)
2 cups milk
2 pears
1/3 cup raisins
Grated peel of 1 lemon
1/2 teaspoon ground cinnamon
1 tablespoon brown sugar
1 egg, separated
3 tablespoons butter

Preheat oven to 350F (175C). Put macaroni and milk in a saucepan. Bring to a boil; reduce heat. Simmer 10 minutes or until macaroni is tender and milk is absorbed. Remove from heat. Peel and core 1 pear. Chop coarsely; add to macaroni with raisins, lemon peel, cinnamon, brown sugar and egg yolk. In a small bowl, whisk egg white until stiff. Gently fold into macaroni mixture. Pour into a greased baking dish. Bake 30 minutes. Peel and core remaining pear. Cut into slices lengthwise. Arrange decoratively around edge of pudding. In a saucepan, melt butter. Brush over pears. Return to the oven for 10 minutes or until pear slices are brown. Makes 4 servings.

Chocolate Spaghetti & White Chocolate Sauce

2 oz. semisweet chocolate, melted, cooled
2 eggs
1-3/4 cups bread flour
Chocolate rosettes, if desired

White Chocolate Sauce:
2 oz. white chocolate
2/3 cup whipping cream

Add melted chocolate to eggs. Make pasta, page 51, using chocolate-egg mixture and bread flour. Let rest 30 minutes. Roll out pasta. Roll pasta sheets through a spaghetti cutter. Put a towel over back of a chair. Spread spaghetti out; let dry 30 minutes. In a large pan of boiling water, cook spaghetti until just tender to the bite. Drain spaghetti. Make sauce. Serve spaghetti with sauce. Garnish with chocolate rosettes, if desired. Makes 4 servings.

To make sauce: Put white chocolate and cream into a saucepan over low heat. Cook, stirring constantly, until chocolate is melted and smooth.

Pasta Meringue Pudding

3/4 cup ditalina (4 oz.)
About 1-3/4 cups milk
1/3 cup powdered sugar
Grated peel of 1 orange
2 eggs, separated
2 tablespoons butter
Kumquat segments, if desired
Angelica leaves, if desired

Put ditalina and 1-3/4 cups milk into a medium-size saucepan. Bring to a boil; reduce heat. Simmer gently 20 minutes or until pasta is tender and milk has been absorbed, adding more milk if necessary. Preheat oven to 300F (150C). Add 5 teaspoons of powdered sugar, orange peel and egg yolks to pasta. Stir well. In a small saucepan, melt butter. Add to pasta mixture. Pour into a greased baking dish. In a bowl, whisk egg whites until stiff. Whisk in all but 1 teaspoon of remaining powdered sugar. Spoon or pipe meringue over pasta mixture. Sprinkle with remaining 1 teaspoon of powdered sugar. Bake 30 minutes or until golden brown and crisp. Decorate with kumquat sections and angelica leaves, if desired. Makes 4 servings.

INDEX